THE **BASICS** OF
ANIMAL
SYSTEMS

THE **BASICS** OF ANIMAL SYSTEMS

ANNE WANJIE, EDITOR

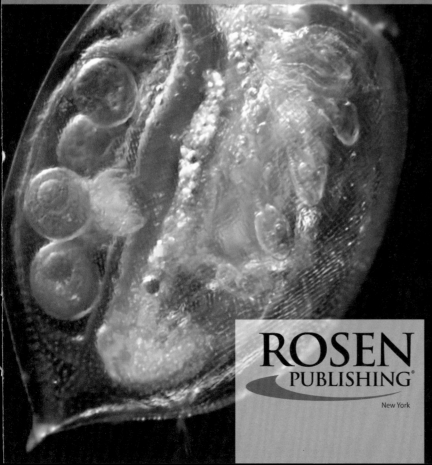

ROSEN
PUBLISHING®
New York

This edition published in 2014 by:

The Rosen Publishing Group, Inc.
29 East 21st Street
New York, NY 10010

Additional end matter copyright © 2014 by The Rosen Publishing Group, Inc.

Library of Congress Cataloging-in-Publication Data

Wanjie, Anne.
The basics of animal systems/by Anne Wanjie.
    p. cm.—(Core concepts)
Includes bibliographical references and index.
ISBN 978-1-4777-0556-8 (library binding)
1. Animals—Variation—Juvenile literature. 2. Animals—Juvenile literature. 3. Biology—Juvenile literature. I. Title.
QL49.W36 2014
507—d23

Manufactured in the United States of America

CPSIA Compliance Information: Batch #S13YA: For further information, contact Rosen Publishing, New York, New York, at 1-800-237-9932.

© 2004 Brown Bear Books Ltd.

CONTENTS

CHAPTER ONE

DIVERSITY IN THE ANIMAL KINGDOM

Animals occur in practically every habitat on Earth. Some filter food; others munch plants or catch other animals.

A camouflaged killer; this flower mantis is colored just like the orchid on which it waits for insect prey.

Biologists divide all living things into vast groups called kingdoms. There are five kingdoms of life: Plants, animals, fungi, bacteria, and protists, though recent research suggests there may be many more. Animals form the kingdom Animalia. Kingdoms are divided further into large groups called phyla (sing. phylum). Each phylum is separated into classes, then orders, families, genera, and species.

TYPES OF SYMMETRY

Most animals are symmetrical. Their body parts match in size, shape, and position on either side of an imaginary line running through an animal.

There are two main types of symmetry in animals. Most, including worms, fish, and humans, are bilaterally symmetrical.

An imaginary line running down the middle of a person's body divides two halves that are mirror images of each

LIFE WITHOUT A GUT

Almost all animals have guts, but a few species manage without. Beard worms live on hydrothermal vents deep underwater. Cavities inside the worms house colonies of bacteria. The worms take chemicals from the waters around them.

The bacteria break down the chemicals. That allows them to produce sugars that feed the worm in return for a safe home. Most parasitic worms also lack guts of their own. Tapeworms (right), for example, live inside the guts of other animals. Bathed in a sea of nutrient-rich liquid, the worms simply absorb food through their skins.

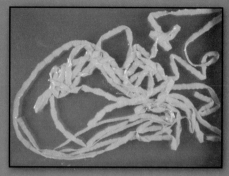

DESCRIBING ANIMALS

Despite their tremendous diversity, all animals share a number of common features. Animals are multicellular organisms—they are formed of many cells that usually form a series of tissues and organs. Animal cells do not have rigid cell walls as those of plants do. Almost all animals possess a gut because they cannot make their own food, as plants can, and must eat to obtain energy. Most animals also have a nervous system that allows them to respond quickly to their environment.

Animals vary enormously in structure, feeding habits, reproduction, and other. Animals such as starfish and jellyfish are different. They have a central axis around which body parts radiate. This is called radial symmetry. A few animals, such as sponges, are not symmetrical at all and take an irregular shape.

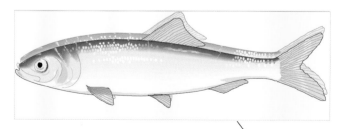

This fish is bilaterally symmetrical. Cleaving the fish along its middle from head to tail leaves two identical halves.

plane of symmetry

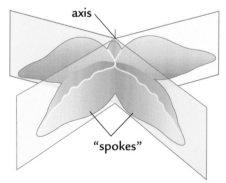

axis

"spokes"

behavior. Their lifestyle as adults may be freeliving, sessile (stay in one place throughout their adult lives, like corals), or parasitic (living in or on another creature). Animals may live in groups, like ants, wildebeest, and prairie dogs, or live alone, seeking a partner only for breeding, as cougars and moose do.

ANIMALS WITHOUT BACKBONES

Most animals are invertebrates—they do not have a backbone. Take a look in your backyard, and you will see invertebrates all around: snails clustering at the bases of plants, earthworms in the soil, and butterflies flapping overhead. There are around 25 invertebrate phyla, including mollusks, echinoderms (starfish and

Jellyfish, such as these moon jellyfish, are among the simplest of all animals. Nonetheless, they have nervous and digestive systems, and a sophisticated venom-delivery system. They use it to kill prey such as other invertebrates and fish.

relatives), and a variety of worms. The simplest invertebrates are placozoans, which consist of just a few thousand cells. Sponges are larger and contain

WHY ARE THERE NO GIANT INSECTS?

In terms of numbers insects are the most successful group in the history of life on Earth. However, even the largest insects are no bigger than around 6 inches (15cm) long. Biologists think that is because of the way they breathe. Insects do not have lungs as people do; instead, they have a system of tubes called tracheae. The tracheae carry oxygen from the air to every cell in their bodies. This system becomes inefficient in larger animals, placing a size limit on these creatures. However, in the past there was more oxygen in the atmosphere. Three hundred million years ago giant invertebrates thrived. They included a scorpion 2.5 feet (76cm) long, a 20-inch- (50cm) long spider, and a giant dragonfly with a 2-foot (60cm) wingspan.

This dragonfly would be dwarfed by its ancient relatives.

millions of cells. Their cells carry out different functions but do not form organs. Jellyfish are more advanced. They have organs and nerve cells so they can respond to the surroundings.

Some invertebrate phyla are very small. The recently discovered Cycliophora, for example, contains just a single tiny species that lives on the lips of Norway lobsters. By contrast, other phyla contain enormous numbers of species. Mollusks include animals as different as clams, slugs, and squid. The most diverse of all animal groups, though, are the arthropods. They include animals such as crabs, spiders, and centipedes, plus the largest group of all, the insects. There are at least 2 million species of insects, but there may be 10 million or more yet to be discovered.

ANIMALS WITH BACKBONES

One phylum of the animal kingdom called the Chordata includes a group of animals that have a hard internal skeleton and a backbone. They are called vertebrates. The backbone protects the spinal cord, which carries signals between head and body.

There are five main groups of vertebrates. They are fish, amphibians, reptiles, birds, and mammals. There is an amazing variety of vertebrate shapes and sizes. Fish called dwarf gobies are just 0.3 inches (8mm) long and weigh less than 0.04 ounces (0.1g). By contrast, blue whales can reach 108 feet (33m) long and weigh up to 135 tons!

Early vertebrates were ocean dwellers. They did not have jaws. Today, just two kinds of jawless vertebrates remain, hagfish and lampreys. Lampreys attach to

LEARNING TO LOVE HAGFISH

The earliest vertebrates looked like hagfish (right). These creatures live in the ocean depths, where they feed on dead animals drifting down from above. Hagfish have no jaws, but they can tear food from a carcass by tying their bodies into a knot and pulling hard. Hagfish have an amazing defense mechanism. A threatened hagfish produces vast quantities of slimy mucus that deters any predator.

larger fish, gouge a hole with their teeth, and drink their blood.

FISH GROUPS AND AMPHIBIANS

Vertebrates include three main fish groups—sharks, ray-finned fish, and lobe-finned fish. Shark skeletons are made of cartilage rather than bone. Ray-finned fish include the largest vertebrate group, the bony fish, with more than 27,000 species. Lobe-finned fish include just the lungfish and coelacanths, but their ancestors were the first vertebrates to move onto land from the sea around 375 million years ago.

Those ancient lobe-finned fish evolved into amphibians, which today include animals such as salamanders, frogs, and toads. Amphibians have moist skins that soon dry out, so they usually live close to water, and their eggs need to be laid in water.

SCALY-SKINNED VERTEBRATES: REPTILES

Reptiles evolved from amphibians. Reptiles have shelled eggs and tough, waterproof skins that allow them to range far from water. Crocodiles are the largest living reptiles; the estuarine crocodile can reach almost 23 feet (7m) long and weighs more than a ton.

Crocodiles lay eggs in nests on land. By contrast, some lizards and snakes give birth to live young. Snakes are one of the most recent reptile groups to evolve. Boas and pythons kill prey by wrapping around it to constrict its breathing. Other snakes, such as rattlesnakes, inject venom through their hollow fangs.

Bony fish are the most diverse of all vertebrate groups. Many, such as these blue stripe snapper, which are reef fish, live in shoals, though others, such as flatfish and cardinalfish, live alone on the sea bottom or among coral.

RETURN OF THE COELACANTH

In 1938 a biologist named Marjorie Courtenay-Latimer (born 1907) noticed a large, strange fish among the catch brought in by some African fishermen. This fish was eventually recognized as a coelacanth, an ancient group thought to have died out 60 million years ago. The fish was given the scientific name *Latimeria* in honor of the woman who spotted it. Since then many coelacanths have been caught off southern Africa and Indonesia. They are lobe-finned fish, close relatives of land-dwelling vertebrates.

BIRDS

All reptiles, amphibians, fish, and invertebrates are cold-blooded—the temperature of their bodies depends on that of their surroundings. Birds are warm-blooded and can maintain their own body temperature. Around 170 million years ago birds evolved from reptiles called dinosaurs, which may also have been warm-blooded.

Birds have feathers that help them retain heat. Their front legs form wings used for flight. Birds must be light, so they have hollow bones and lay eggs instead of carrying young inside their bodies. Birds also have air sacs in the body to increase airflow to the lungs and a strong heart to keep cells supplied with oxygen-rich blood.

The forelimbs of birds, such as this ring-billed gull, have evolved into wings used for powered flight.

WARM-BLOODED VERTEBRATES: MAMMALS

Birds are not the only group of warm-blooded animals to have evolved from reptiles. Mammals evolved from a different reptile group, the therapsids. There are about 5,000 species of mammals today, including kangaroos, mice, humans, and our closest relatives, apes and monkeys. Rather than feathers, mammals have hair that saves body heat. Two species, the platypus and the echidna, lay eggs, but all other mammals give birth to live young. Female mammals nurse their young and feed them milk.

This is an echidna, or spiny anteater. Echidnas live only in Australia and New Guinea. They, along with the platypus, are the only living mammals that lay eggs.

CHAPTER TWO

WAYS OF EATING

FILTER FEEDERS

Animals as different as flamingos (below), sponges, and clams are all filter feeders. They draw in water using their beaks, gills, or other body parts and strain off tiny creatures called plankton to eat. Baleen whales such as blue whales are also filter feeders. They sieve small shrimplike animals called krill from water with a fringe of huge baleen plates in their mouths.

All animals need energy for fuel and nutrients to build and repair their bodies. They get these vital raw materials from their food.

The millions of species of animals can be divided by the different ways they feed. Carnivores, like sharks, spiders, and wolves, eat other animals, while herbivores such as cows and rabbits eat plants. Herbivores may eat a wide range of plant foods or specialize in just one. Koalas, for example, feed only on eucalyptus leaves.

Biologists call animals that eat both plant and animal food omnivores. They include foxes, raccoons, and people. Other animals called filter feeders sieve tiny plants and animals from water, while detritivores feed on dead and decaying matter.

Plant food is often easy to gather, but it is less nourishing than meat. Animals

SURPRISE OMNIVORES

People often think of pandas as peaceful animals that eat nothing but bamboo. Pandas are members of the order Carnivora and are related to bears, cats, and dogs. Pandas switched to an herbivorous diet millions of years ago. However, when a panda stumbles on the body of a dead animal, it reveals its meat-eating ancestry by feasting on the rotting flesh. Many other herbivorous animals switch to meat when it is easily available. Fruit-eating duiker antelopes will sometimes catch insects and small mammals, while hippos, which usually feed on grasses, will eat dead animals. Similarly, praying mantises will switch from catching insects to munching fruit when prey is in short supply.

that eat leaves may have to spend many hours feeding. Koalas, for example, feed for up to 18 hours each day. Other plant foods, such as nuts, seeds, and fruits, are more nourishing. Mice and squirrels hoard such foods for times when food is scarce.

Filter feeders also spend much of their time eating. Prey is difficult to find and catch, but it is nourishing, so carnivores can survive for longer between meals.

EVOLUTION OF FEEDING

Over long periods of time animals have evolved many features that help them feed. These are called adaptations. Herbivores, for example, have mouthparts and digestive systems that have evolved to cope with tough plant food. Water animals that eat algae, such as limpets and parrotfish,

A raccoon is an omnivore. It can eat meat, as well as fruit and seeds, dead material, and even trash from people's garbage cans.

HOW DO BIRDS FEED?

Birds that visit your backyard eat different foods so they do not compete with each other. Find out about local birds' feeding habits by putting out a range of foods, such as nuts, seeds, cheese, and bacon rind. Which birds prefer each food, and how are their beaks suited to their feeding habits? This is called a food-preference survey.

FEASTING ON THE DEAD

Scavenging is a good way to get meat without running the risk of catching dangerous, well-armed prey. Hyenas, jackals, and vultures are all expert scavengers. Other carnivores, such as lions and crocodiles, as well as opportunists like crows and raccoons, will eat dead animals given the chance. Scavengers pick off injured and dying animals or feed on rotting meat and tough parts of prey left behind by other hunters. Hyenas have strong jaws and teeth that can crush bones and slice through tough gristle. Lammergeier vultures get to tasty bone marrow in a different way. They carry bones high in the air and then drop them onto the rocks below.

A spotted hyena scavenges for scraps from the rotting carcass of a zebra.

have rasping mouthparts with which they scrape their food off rocks. Mammals that eat plants have flat-topped teeth for grinding, and some, such as cows, have stomachs with many chambers to help them digest food efficiently.

Plant eaters as diverse as antelopes, sheep, and termites have tiny

SINK OR SWIM

Many animals live and feed within the guts of people. These parasites must avoid being washed out of the body with food. Tapeworms wedge their spiny head (or scolex) into the gut wall. Giant nematodes do not anchor themselves, but instead swim against the tide of food—they may swim up as far as the throat.

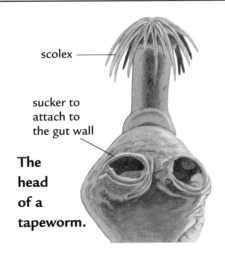

scolex

sucker to attach to the gut wall

The head of a tapeworm.

DISCOVER DETRITIVORES

Soil-dwelling organisms such as mites, millipedes, and earthworms play a vital role in recycling nutrients. They are detritivores, which feed on dung and decaying plant and animal matter. To study these animals, try making this simple piece of equipment: Cut the bottom from a plastic pot, and replace it with some fine wire mesh. Put the pot into a funnel, and put some decaying leaves and topsoil onto the mesh. Put the funnel in a jar containing water, and direct a strong light onto the soil. The animals in the soil will move away from the light and drop into the jar. You will need a magnifying glass to see the detritivores.

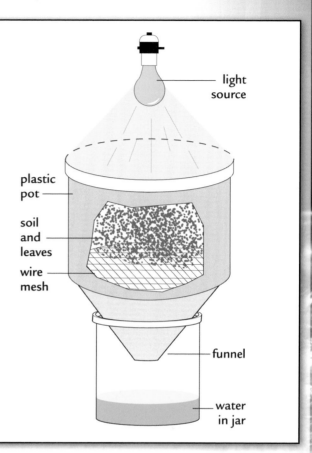

light source

plastic pot

soil and leaves

wire mesh

funnel

water in jar

microorganisms in their guts. They help break down a tough material called cellulose, which occurs in plant leaves and stems.

The bodies of carnivores are also suited to their feeding habits. Predatory (hunting) mammals such as lions and hyenas have powerful jaws and jagged teeth that grip and slice their food into chunks that can be swallowed. Birds such as eagles and falcons have sharp claws to grip prey and powerful hooked beaks to rip it to pieces.

THE SENSES OF SIGHT AND HEARING

Predators rely on their sharp senses to track down their food. Herbivores also need a keen awareness of their surroundings to stay one step ahead of predators. Animals possess the same range of senses that people have. They are sight, smell, hearing, taste, and touch.

For people sight is the most important sense, yet hunters such as hawks have much keener vision. Wolves and

INSECT SENSES

Many insects find their food using antennae. They are feelers used for detecting chemicals and for touch. Flies have taste sensors on their feet. Most adult insects have large compound eyes made up of many lenses, each of which produces a tiny image. The insect's brain pieces the images together to build up a bigger picture. Insects can see ultraviolet light, which is invisible to humans. That helps them find nectar in flowers, which often have ultraviolet markers to show where nectar stores are.

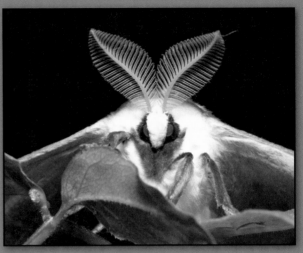

This luna moth has compound eyes to see and fringed antennae to detect chemicals.

sharks rely more on smell—detection of chemicals—when tracking down prey. Predators such as owls can hear very faint sounds that our ears cannot detect. For many animals vision is of little use for finding food at night. Small bats use sound instead. This is called echolocation. The bats produce high-pitched squeaks that bounce off objects such as moths. The bat listens for the echoes to pinpoint the prey. Most larger bats, called fruit bats, do not echolocate. They rely on smell and enormous eyes to find fruit to eat.

SENSING SMELLS AND VIBRATIONS

Your dog knows your neighborhood in a different way than you do. Humans rely on familiar sights to find their way. Your dog follows a familiar pattern of smells instead.

OTHER ECHOLOCATORS

It is not just insect-eating bats that echolocate to find food. Dolphins use underwater clicks to find fish in murky waters. Their powers of echolocation are amazing; they can detect a small ball just an inch across from more than 230 feet (70 m) away! Some other animals that forage for food at night or in dark waters also echolocate, including killer whales, birds called cave swiftlets, and some seals and shrews.

Smells are also important for other hunting animals. A snake gathers chemicals from the air with its flicking tongue. The chemicals are passed to a sensitive organ in the roof of the snake's mouth. Snakes use sound, too. They lack ears, but sound vibrations traveling through the ground make a tiny bone move so the snake can still detect the sounds. Scorpions also track prey by detecting vibrations; their sensors are on their feet. Fish sense vibrations in water using a sensory strip running down their bodies called a lateral line.

EXTRAORDINARY SENSES

Some animals possess "super senses" that humans lack. For example, snakes can detect the body heat of prey such as mice using sensitive pits in their cheeks. That allows snakes to hunt at night. In the oceans sharks and eels track prey using electric fields. Animals such as whales, bees, pigeons, and turtles can sense Earth's magnetic field. That helps them find their way as they travel over long distances.

AT HOME IN THE DARK

Human eyesight is of little use in the dark, but many nocturnal (night-active) animals have eyes that make the most of dim light to help them find food. Take a look at a cat at night. Light passing through its eye bounces back off a reflective layer behind the retina. That doubles the amount of light that can be absorbed. The reflected light gives cats' eyes an eerie greenish glow. Nocturnal primates, such as bushbabies, do things differently. They have huge eyes that capture as much light as possible. These animals have no need for color vision; they see their world in black and white.

The lesser bushbaby is about to munch on some tasty fruit.

FEEDING ON PREY

Once a victim has been found, predators need a way to subdue and kill it. Many use sharp teeth and claws, but some small predators use venom instead. Jellyfish, sea anemones, and corals have tentacles with stinging cells that they use to paralyze small animals. Spiders and centipedes bite their prey and inject venom through their fangs. Snakes such as cobras

A song thrush prepares to smash open a snail shell on a rock, or "anvil." Each song thrush has a favorite anvil; the ground around it can become littered with shell fragments.

SNAKE VENOM

The venoms of many snakes contain chemicals called neurotoxins. They attack the victim's nervous system. The neurotoxins prevent signals from the animal's brain reaching its muscles, so it becomes paralyzed. In laboratories captive snakes are "milked" for their venom (right). The venom is used to make a snake bite antidote. Biologists have learned to make drugs that mimic the effect of snake neurotoxins. These drugs are given to patients to relax their muscles before surgery.

use venoms that are powerful enough to kill a person, while wasps and scorpions paralyze their prey using venomous stingers on their tails.

Prey animals have a range of defenses against enemies, but some hunters have learned to overcome them. For example, a snail's shell protects it against most enemies, but thrushes are able to smash snails against stones to get at the soft-bodied creatures inside. Porcupines are covered with prickly quills that deter most predators. However, carnivorous mammals called fishers can defeat them by attacking their heads, which have few quills. Similarly, some mice can overcome the lethal chemical jets released by bombardier beetles by plunging the beetles tail-first into mud.

FISHING AS A TEAM

Humpback whales off the coast of Alaska feed in an unusual and sophisticated way. Groups of around seven whales gather below a school of herring. The whales coordinate their positions relative to each other with high-pitched screams—these sounds also terrify and confuse the fish. Next, the whales breathe out enormous bubbles of water that rise to the surface. The bubbles act as a net, forcing the herring closer and closer together. Finally, the whales plunge up through the bubbles with their mouths wide open (below).
The fish are caught in huge numbers. They are strained from the water by baleen plates in the whale's mouth before being swallowed.

HUNTING IN GROUPS

Lions, wolves, African hunting dogs, and killer whales are predators that cooperate when hunting. Cooperation allows them to target larger victims than they could manage on their own. A pack may spread out to surround a victim or take turns chasing and tiring it. A lion hunting alone only kills 15 percent of the animals it targets. Two to four lions more than double this success rate, killing successfully on 32 percent of hunts.

PURSUING PREY

In the natural world predators use a variety of techniques to capture their victims. Top predators such as lions, falcons, and crocodiles mainly ambush their prey. Cheetahs quietly stalk prey such as gazelles to get within range before attacking. They mainly target young, sickly, or old animals since they are the easiest victims to catch. Even so, cheetahs are often unsuccessful in their attacks.

Wolves and African hunting dogs do things differently. They work in groups to chase prey down slowly—these animals can pursue their quarry over any terrain for many hours until it tires.

Smaller predators usually rely on stealth rather than speed to capture their prey. They may simply lie in wait for passing animals. Some, such as frogs and chameleons, grab insect prey using their very long, very sticky tongues. Trapdoor spiders dash out of their burrows to grab insects, detecting them through an intricate network of silken tripwires around the entrance.

Other small hunters set traps, pits, or snares for their victims.

This toad has used its long, sticky tongue to snatch a tasty earthworm. The tip of the tongue leaves the mouth, sticks to the worm, and returns to the mouth in an incredible 0.07 seconds.

PREY-FOOLING CAMOUFLAGE

Animals that lie in wait for prey are often camouflaged, with body colors that match their surroundings. Victims do not see them until too late. Flower mantises are predatory insects that closely resemble flowers called orchids. They wait motionless for passing insects, then grab them with their front legs and eat them. Wobbegong sharks (below) live in seas around Australia. They have speckles, blotches, and fringes on their bodies that blend in with the seabed. The sharks lurk on the bottom and snap up any creatures that come within range.

Ant lions dig pits in sand and wait for smaller insects to fall in, while orb-web spiders weave silken snares to catch flying insects.

Anglerfish are predators with an amazing hunting aid. They attract small fish using a built-in lure. It is a long spine with a fleshy lobe on the end that looks like a worm. This tasty-looking bait dangles in front of the angler's jaws. When a fish comes close to nibble the "worm," the anglerfish pounces.

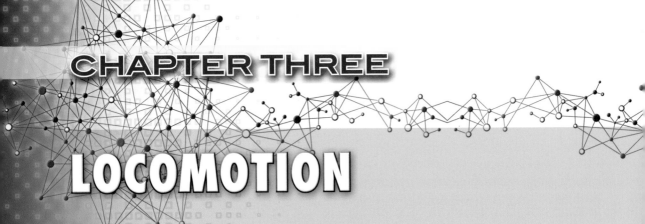

CHAPTER THREE

LOCOMOTION

Most animals need to move at some stage in their lives. It may be to look for food sources, to find a mate, or to escape competitors or predators.

Animal locomotion (movement) depends on the properties of muscles. They are bundles of fibers that contract to convert energy into movement. To raise your arm, for example, your bicep muscle contracts. Muscles cannot work without something to anchor to. Most human muscles anchor to bones, though some, such as the muscles in your tongue, anchor against other muscles. Insect muscles are anchored to their tough outer shells, or exoskeletons.

A FLUID–FILLED CAVITY

Many animals brace their muscles against a hydrostatic skeleton. It is a fluid-filled cavity inside the animal's body. The pressure of the fluid acts as an anchor for the muscles around it. The hydrostatic skeleton of an earthworm, for example, is divided into segments. They allow the animal to push through dirt.

Other animals with hydrostatic skeletons loop around. Leeches have just one body cavity. They attach to the ground with suckers at each

This incredible animal is called a basilisk. These lizards can run across the surface of a pond or river to escape predators.

end of their bodies, then loop around the pivot.

JET POWER

Some animals use hydrostatic skeletons to swim. These animals are jet powered. They squirt water in one direction, and the force propels them in the opposite direction. Jellyfish and squid are jet propelled. Dragonfly nymphs draw water into their rear ends and squirt it out to move quickly through the water. Scallops swim using a pair of jets on either side of their shell hinge.

Jet propulsion is good for short bursts of fast swimming to escape a predator

HOW WORMS GET AROUND

The earthworm body cavity is divided into many segments. They help the worm inch through dirt. The worm uses muscles to narrow segments that thrust through the soil. Then the segment expands. It lodges in the dirt with bristly hairs so the worm can pull itself forward.

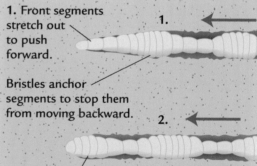

1. Front segments stretch out to push forward.

Bristles anchor segments to stop them from moving backward.

2. Segments shorten, pulling other segments forward.

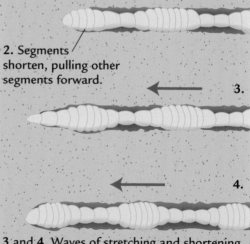

3 and 4. Waves of stretching and shortening allow the worm to inch along.

This dragonfly nymph has caught a minnow. These nymphs use jet propulsion to move quickly underwater. When they complete their development, they leave the water, molt to reveal wings, and fly away.

or grab prey, but it is less efficient at low speeds. Squid, for example, usually get around by flapping fins that run along the sides of their bodies.

MOTION WITH FINS

Fish also use fins to swim. Slow swimming is powered by small red muscles that run through their trunks. For bursts of fast swimming fish use powerful banks of white muscles. Muscles contract to flex the body of a fish from side to side. In fish like eels this causes a ripple along the body. In other types of fish, such as goldfish, most of the side-to-side movement comes from the tail. Whales and dolphins also use their tails to drive themselves forward, though these mammals flap their tails up and down.

A third group of fish, mainly ones that live on reefs or in kelp beds, use their front fins as paddles to row through the water. Many other underwater animals, such as seals and turtles, are also rowers.

CRAWLING CREEPERS

Crawling animals such as slugs need mucus to move. Slugs crawl on their large,

WALK ON WATER

Take a look at a pond in summer, and you will see many small animals on the surface. They may include water striders (left), water measurers, whirligig beetles, and even fishing spiders. All these animals depend on a property of water called surface tension. It creates an elastic "skin" on the water surface. Very light creatures with water-repelling hairs on their feet can skim across this skin. A few larger animals also walk on water. Basilisks are lizards that run across water to escape predators. They do this by slapping their feet down hard and fast—they must take 20 steps each second to stay afloat!

You might think the trail of sticky mucus left by a snail is nasty, but these animals would be unable to crawl from place to place without it. Snail mucus is mostly water, but it also contains proteins that give it curious properties.

muscular foot, secreting sticky mucus from glands as they go. Waves of muscular movement run along the foot. However, the slug does not lift its foot—the mucus is too sticky to allow that. Instead, mucus acts like a solid against which the foot can push. But when the foot pushes hard enough, the mucus changes its properties to act like a liquid. That allows part of the foot to glide forward. As the pressure drops off, the mucus switches back to behaving like a solid, and the process is repeated.

WALKERS AND RUNNERS

To get around on land, many animals walk or run. Cold-blooded animals such as amphibians and reptiles have powerful bursts of activity. A crocodile leaps from the water to snatch a drinking antelope; frogs can hop explosively to avoid a predator. However, these animals are unable to sustain their

bursts of activity for long. The champion runners over longer distances are the warm-blooded mammals. Although you may think mammals like cats, horses, mice, and dogs move around in different ways, their movements are actually very similar. The way an animal moves its legs is called its gait.

Gaits differ according to how fast an animal is moving. A horse walks slowly, speeds up to a trot, and eventually breaks into a run. A mouse does exactly the same thing, although at much lower speeds.

A Nile crocodile attacks a wildebeest. Reptiles and amphibians are capable of bursts of powerful activity. However, unlike birds and mammals, these animals are unable to sustain fast movement for long.

CHEETAH CHEATS

It is well known that the fastest land animal is the cheetah. Look in most textbooks, and you will probably read that this cat's top speed is 70 mph (112 km/h). However, this figure is incorrect and is based on a poorly conducted experiment of the 1950s. More accurate measurements made in 1997 reveal a top speed of 63 mph (102 km/h)—still mighty impressive, but lower than the false value accepted as fact for many years.

People switch gaits from walking to running at about 5 miles per hour (8 km/h). Birds also change gaits as they switch from slow to faster flapping flight.

ELASTIC QUALITIES

Saving energy during movement is very important. Many structures inside animals have elastic properties. They store energy as they move, then release it, so the animal uses less overall. Kangaroos

Elastic tendons in this kangaroo's legs help it save energy as it bounds.

have elastic tendons in their legs that snap back after they are stretched, like a rubber band. Around 40 percent of the energy used by kangaroos for hopping is saved in this way.

A much more efficient elastic material, resilin, occurs in the bodies of flying insects. Insects use muscles to pull down the exoskeleton (outer surface) of their midbody. That makes the

HOW FAST DID DINOSAURS RUN?

Since dinosaurs died out millions of years ago, you might think figuring out how fast they could run would be an impossible task. However, English biologist Neill Alexander (born 1934) managed just that. Using modern animals, Alexander figured out how to predict an animal's speed from the distance between its footprints and the length of the leg from foot to hip.

Alexander's equations suggest that huge long-necked dinosaurs such as Brachiosaurus walked at around 7.5 mph (12 km/h). Large meat-eating theropods such as Tyrannosaurus rex could run at up to 12.5 mph (20 km/h).

HITCHING A RIDE

A great way to save energy while moving from place to place is to let another animal do all the work. Flower mites feed on flower nectar. Since they are tiny, getting to new food sources is a problem. The mites wait for a hummingbird to visit their flower. Then they dash up its bill and wriggle into the bird's nostrils. They clamber back down the bill when the bird finds another flower to feed from.

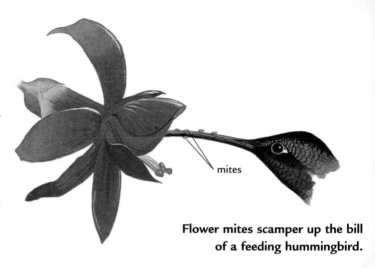
mites

Flower mites scamper up the bill of a feeding hummingbird.

wings move up. Resilin in the exoskeleton helps pull the wings down again. The insect can do this without having to use more energy moving muscles.

GLIDING ANIMALS

Imagine a tree-living animal foraging in the forest. To save energy and avoid a trip across the ground, it makes sense to glide between the trees. Gliding has evolved many times in various animal groups. There are gliding lizards, mammals, frogs, and even fish and squid, and there were once gliding dinosaurs too. To glide, an animal needs a surface on its body that acts as a wing.

FLAPPING FLIGHT

Unlike gliding, powered (or flapping) flight has evolved just a few times, in

WHAT'S WRONG WITH WHEELS?

Most human transportation depends on wheels, on trains, carts, and automobiles. But despite their efficiency, wheels do not occur in nature. That may be due to the difficulty of getting nutrients into structures that spin in circles. Also, wheels are only of use on flat, relatively smooth surfaces—they cannot run over bumps of more than around a quarter of their width. A few animals, though, overcome these problems and roll their entire bodies into a wheel shape to escape predators. Some dune spiders curl into a ball and let the wind carry them across the sand. Similarly, some cliff caterpillars form a loop with their bodies, then tumble down the rock face.

GLIDING THROUGH THE AIR

For animals that glide or fly, wing shape is critical. A wing forms a shape called an airfoil (below). Air pouring over the top surface of an airfoil moves more quickly than air sliding beneath its lower surface. That creates a difference in air pressure that sucks the wing upward, creating a force called lift. Lift opposes the weight of the animal, which pulls the animal downward. But lift alone cannot overcome another force called drag, caused by the resistance of the air to movement through it.

Drag places a limit on how far a gliding animal can go; to remain airborne over a longer distance, an animal must be able to flap its wings.

The wings of a flying squirrel are formed by thin flaps of skin. They make an airfoil, enabling the animal to glide.

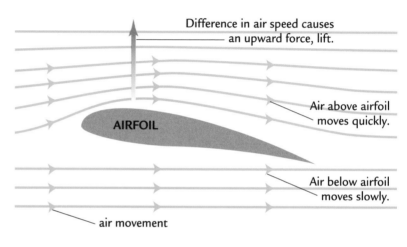

Difference in air speed causes an upward force, lift.

AIRFOIL

Air above airfoil moves quickly.

Air below airfoil moves slowly.

air movement

birds, insects, bats, and in extinct reptiles called pterosaurs. Flapping wings allow an animal such as a bird to overcome the effects of drag (see box above), so they can travel much farther than any glider.

Although flight uses more energy than any other form of movement, flying animals have many advantages over ground-based creatures. They can fly to catch food, escape predators, or migrate vast distances. The type of flight depends on the shape of the

A ladybug in flight. Flight enables insects to find food, escape predators, and travel over long distances.

MOVEMENTS OF AIR

Why do animals like birds and butterflies flap their wings? Flapping provides a force—thrust—that acts in combination with lift to overcome the forces of gravity and drag. Each time a small bird flaps its wings, swirls of air called vortices leave the wing (right). They roll up into doughnut shapes that trail behind the animal as it flies, though people cannot see them, of course. These doughnuts, or vortex rings, also form behind flapping bats and insects. For larger birds with pointed wings, such as gulls and hawks, a different type of vortex forms. It is a tube of swirling air that follows the path of the wingtips.

Each time the macaw makes a downstroke with its wings (left), a vortex ring is produced in the air behind the bird.

flying macaw

The forces that operate on a bird flying from left to right and their directions (below).

lift

drag ← → thrust

gravity

vortex ring

Hold a piece of paper horizontally from your lips. It will droop a little, but start blowing gently across its top surface. What happens to the paper? Bearing in mind what you have learned about animal flight, what do you think is happening here? See the box on 28 for a clue.

UNDERSTANDING LIFT

Hold a piece of paper horizontally from your lips. It will droop a little, but start blowing gently across its top surface. What happens to the paper? Bearing in mind what you have learned about animal flight, what do you think is happening here? See the box on 28 for a clue.

wings. Long wings, such as those of dragonflies and hawks, allow maneuverable flight. Shorter wings are better for faster flight, while large, long wings, such as those of albatrosses and vultures, help birds glide on rising air currents. That helps them fly many miles without wasting energy on flapping.

CHAPTER FOUR

ADAPTING TO HABITATS

Emperor penguins raise their chicks on the coast of Antarctica, one of the most inhospitable places on Earth.

Animals live almost everywhere on Earth—in rivers, lakes, and oceans, in the air, on land, and in the soil.

The type of place where an animal lives is called its habitat. Animals like rats, foxes, and cockroaches are generalists—adaptable creatures able to thrive in many habitats. Most animals, however, are adapted to live in just one particular habitat and cannot survive elsewhere. For example, most penguins are suited to life in and around cold southern seas, and could not survive in a desert. Some animals begin life in one environment and move to another as adults. Adult toads can live on land, but they develop from water-dwelling tadpoles.

HIBERNATION AND DIAPAUSE

In temperate and cool climates many animals ride out harsh winter weather by entering the deep sleep of hibernation. Body processes such as heart rate and breathing slow down, and the animal's body temperature drops dramatically. This strategy saves energy that would otherwise be lost searching for scarce food in the cold. When the weather warms

AMAZING MIGRATIONS

Many animals avoid harsh conditions by making long, seasonal journeys called migrations. They may travel thousands of miles to avoid winter weather, find food, or reach a safe place to breed. Caribou, whales, monarch butterflies, salmon, eels, and turtles are all famous migrants. Many North American birds, such as hummingbirds, waders, and geese, migrate south for the winter. The champion migrants, however, are Arctic terns, which fly up to 20,000 miles (32,000km) as they shuttle between the Arctic and Antarctic each year.

The monarch butterfly (right) makes an amazing two-way journey each year (below).

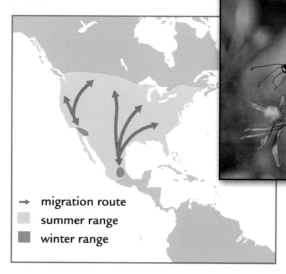

→ migration route
▨ summer range
■ winter range

FRIGID HABITATS

The polar regions are one of the harshest habitats on Earth, with bitterly cold temperatures except during the brief summer and up to six months' darkness each year. Land in these areas is permanently covered with a thick sheet of ice. For much of the year the seas are also ice-covered, but they abound with animals such as whales, seals, and fish. Such diversity relies on plankton, which thrive in the nutrient-rich waters. Polar bears and penguins live

up, the animal becomes active again. Bats, ground squirrels, ormice, snakes, tortoises, and amphibians such as toads hibernate. Many insects enter a similar state of suspension called diapause to help them survive winter, famine, or drought.

This hibernating dormouse is fast asleep in its nest.

ACTIVE ALL YEAR ROUND

The tundra is home to rodents such as lemmings and voles. In temperate lands farther south many rodents hibernate to avoid the winter chill; but surprisingly, few Arctic rodents hibernate. They dig burrows in the soil and through the snow, where temperatures remain higher than above ground. In these burrows the rodents remain active all year round, nibbling the roots of tundra plants.

and breed on floating sea ice or on coasts. However, just a few tiny animals, such as springtails and roundworms, can survive farther inland.

South of the Arctic lie the barren, treeless lowlands of the tundra. Here winters are also long and very cold, but summers are warmer, with long hours of light. Arctic foxes and hares, lemmings, and snowy owls are among the few species that live on the tundra all year round. Other animals, such as caribou, migrate there in spring to breed.

Animals of polar and nearpolar lands have physical features that help them withstand the harsh climate. Mammals such as muskoxen, Arctic foxes, and polar bears have thick, hairy coats. Arctic foxes also have hairy feet and small ears that help conserve body heat. Aquatic

Chamois, rare mountain goats that live in central Europe, are expert climbers.

MOUNTAIN ANIMALS

Conditions high on mountains are similar to polar climates, with freezing temperatures, high winds, and ice and snow underfoot. Different communities of animals occur at different altitudes (heights above sea level) on mountains. The greatest variety live in the foothills. Fewer species live on the summits. Animals such as chamois migrate up and down the mountain to avoid the harshest weather, while marmots and alpine reptiles spend up to six months of the year in hibernation.

creatures such as seals and penguins have thick layers of blubber just under the skin that provide insulation.

DESERT HABITATS

Lack of moisture is the main problem in deserts. They are places that receive less than 10 inches (25cm) of rain each year. These harsh habitats also have extreme variations in temperature. Most deserts are boiling hot by day and freezing cold at night; high-altitude deserts are cold most of the time. Food and shelter are also scarce. Despite this, a surprising number of animals live in deserts, including a range of insects, spiders, scorpions, and reptiles, and also many mammals and birds.

Desert mammals have pale fur that reflects the sun and provides good

This sleeping fennec fox is superbly adapted for desert life. Its pale colors reflect heat and provide camouflage. The fox can lose heat quickly through its enormous ears.

camouflage. Desert hares and foxes have large ears that radiate body heat, helping the animal keep cool, while Cape ground squirrels use their long bushy tails as portable sunshades. Sand cats, addax antelope, and web-footed geckoes have broad

ESTIVATION

Many desert animals spend much of their lives in a state called estivation, a type of summer hibernation. Most amphibians are water-loving animals, but spadefoot toads live in deserts. These toads spend up to ten months of the year fast asleep, buried in the mud of dried-up pools. When rain falls, the toads emerge and spawn in the pools. Their tadpoles grow up faster than those of other amphibians. As the pools dry up again, the young toads dig down into the mud, where they estivate until the rains return.

WHAT ARE BIOMES?

Biomes are vast groupings of habitats. For example, regions in the world with very low rainfalls are grouped into the desert biome. Habitats are more specific. The Sonoran desert, with its giant cacti and other distinctive plants, forms a habitat. Habitats can be broken down too, into microhabitats. Animals living around the roots of giant saguaro cactus live in a microhabitat.

feet to keep them from sinking into the sand. Camels have many adaptations to desert life, including broad feet and long eyelashes to keep out sand. Their single or double hump acts as a fat store. These animals can survive for days without water.

DEW COLLECTORS

Desert creatures such as burrowing owls, lizards, and snakes spend the hot midday hours in cool burrows or in the shade of rocks. They emerge to search for food at dusk, when temperatures drop. Most desert animals get all the moisture they need from their food, so they do not need to drink. However, there is usually some water available in even the driest desert—in the cool of the early morning dew often forms. Some animals can exploit this precious resource. Desert beetles allow dew to collect on their bodies. One of the most effective dew collectors is an Australian lizard called a moloch. This animal is

KEEPING BRINE SHRIMP

Very few animals can live in extremely salty water, but one group of particularly tough animals thrives in such an environment. They are brine shrimp, tiny crustaceans that live in salty lakes such as the Great Salt Lake, Utah. The little shrimp lay eggs called cysts, which can survive being dried out for many years. When the cysts are immersed in water, the young shrimp hatch quickly. Brine shrimp cysts are sold in pet shops. Buy a packet, put the cysts in water, and watch these hardy survivors hatch and grow.

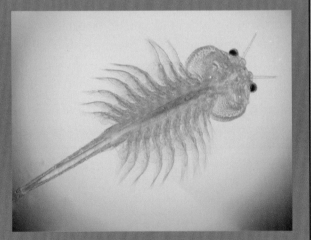

Brine shrimp are filter feeders. They strain bacteria and other tiny organisms from the water.

FABULOUS FEATHERS

Getting enough water is essential for all desert animals. Sandgrouse (right, at a desert pool) can simply fly to regular watering holes, although that may involve journeys of 30 miles (50 km) or more. But how can these birds get water to their chicks, which are unable to leave the nest? Male sandgrouse have feathers on their bellies that act as an extremely efficient sponge. The bird walks into a pool of water and soaks these belly feathers. They absorb water, and the male then flies back to the nest. There the thirsty chicks suck the water from the feathers.

covered with sharp spines to fend off predators. Running along the spines are a series of grooves that channel moisture along the animal's body and into the corner of its mouth.

Grooves running along the spines of a moloch channel water into the thorny lizard's mouth.

FORESTS AS HABITATS

Forests and woodlands offer animals shelter from the elements and good sites to nest and hide from enemies. The abundance of plant life attracts a wide range of plant eaters, which attract predators in turn. The cold pine forests of the north are home to fewer species than temperate woodlands, where trees lose their leaves in fall. In both these habitats food is scarce in winter, so some animals hibernate, while others migrate. Tropical rainforests grow nearer the equator. There the climate is always warm and wet, and plantlife remains lush all year round. Rainforests contain a greater variety of life than any other habitat.

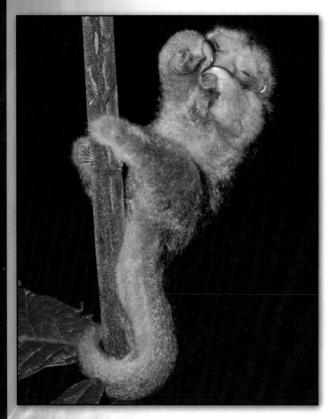

Many mammals of the forest canopy, such as this pygmy anteater from the South American rainforest, use their tails as an extra limb. This helps them cling tightly to tree branches.

Many monkeys and other canopy mammals have a gripping tail that acts as a climbing aid. A few animals, such as flying squirrels, can glide between trees by spreading flaps of skin to act as a wing. Other animals, including deer, pigs, and rodents such as agoutis, are adapted to life on the shady forest floor. They often feed on food dropped by canopy animals or on fruit and seeds that fall from the trees above.

In rainforests the canopy—the layer of leaves highest above the ground—is home to the greatest number of species. Canopy animals are either fliers such as bats, birds, and insects or skilled climbers such as squirrels and monkeys.

ANIMALS IN GRASSLANDS

Grasslands occur naturally in regions that are too dry for forests, yet are moist enough for grasses to grow. The world's biggest grasslands are in east Africa, where large herds of grazing mammals

BE A WOODLAND DETECTIVE

You'll need to do some serious sleuthing to find out about the animals that inhabit a park, forest, or woodland near you. Many woodland creatures are shy or nocturnal (night active), and you are more likely to find the traces they leave behind than glimpse the animals themselves. Look for burrows in the ground made by foxes or holes in trees where woodpeckers nest. Gnawed bark and nuts, droppings, footprints in the mud, and claw marks on trees are all clues to particular woodland species. What animals do you think left the clues you find? A guidebook to local wildlife will help you identify them.

This is a black-footed ferret, among the rarest mammals in North America. Ferrets eat prairie dogs and live in their burrows. The ferrets suffered a great decline as the prairies were transformed into cropland by settlers.

A gray reef shark searches for prey. Sharks are streamlined, an adaptation for fast swimming in pursuit of fish and other underwater animals.

such as zebras and gazelles feed on grasses, while giraffes and elephants browse on isolated trees.

Grasslands offer little cover for animals, so ground squirrels, reptiles, and some birds burrow underground. Tropical grasslands have rainy and dry seasons. Grassland mammals may migrate long distances in search of food and water in the dry season.

ANIMALS IN OCEANS

Oceans provide a variety of habitats for wildlife. Warm, sunlit coastal waters and coral reefs offer favorable conditions, and life can be very abundant in these places. However, underwater life also thrives in less favorable environments, including the open ocean, where there is no place to hide from enemies. Predators such as tuna, sharks, and dolphins hunt shoals of herring and mackerel that feed on plankton there. The gloomy ocean depths are a more

POLLUTION

Human use of the oceans as a dump for all sorts of waste has led to high levels of pollution in the oceans. Coastal waters are often the most polluted because rivers discharge sewage from cities and chemicals from farms and factories there. Farther out to sea oil tankers flush their tanks, and toxic waste and junk are dumped. Marine life of all kinds suffers. In recent years many seas have become so polluted that governments have had to put tight controls on the disposal of waste.

the waters above. The deep sea is also very cold. In polar seas some fish have a natural antifreeze in their blood that prevents their tissues from freezing.

Food in the deep ocean is often scarce. Most animals feed on dead and decaying material drifting down from the waters above. Predators such as gulper eels have huge mouths and stretchy stomachs so they can swallow any prey they come across.

Seashores are also harsh places to live; conditions change constantly. Limpets, mussels, and sea anemones must survive the buffeting of the waves and being

hostile habitat. Fish, starfish, sponges, and other animals there must cope with total darkness and the great pressure caused by

A natural antifreeze flows through the blood of icefish, allowing these unusual animals to thrive in cold polar waters.

SURVIVING EXTREMES

Insects are the hardiest of all animals. Some thrive in conditions that would quickly kill a person. Wetas, giant crickets from New Zealand, can survive being completely frozen during the winter. After thawing in spring, they wander away unharmed.

The masters of extreme survival, though, are brine flies. These insects can live in water up to five times saltier than the ocean. The pools in which they live often reach temperatures of more than 158°F (70°C), while in laboratory conditions the flies can survive at temperatures of up to 392°F (200°C).

A mudskipper can paddle in water or energetically jump on land. It has adapted to an amphibious lifestyle and burrows in mud.

submerged then left high and dry at each turn of the tide.

FRESHWATER ANIMALS

Freshwater rivers, lakes, and swamps make rich habitats for fish, shellfish, amphibians, turtles, waterfowl, and many other animals. Creatures that inhabit fast-flowing streams must be strong swimmers to avoid being swept away. In some aquatic habitats such as swamps the water may become very low in oxygen or even dry up completely. A few fish, such as mudskippers and climbing perch, can survive out of water for a time. A lungfish copes by burrowing into the mud at the bottom of a pool when it begins to dry up. Safely encased in a cocoon of mucus, the lungfish estivates. The fish can survive like this for years, until the pond begins to fill with water again.

POND DIPPING

Check out freshwater life by dipping in a local pond. You will need a small net. Make sure an adult is present to help you. Swish the net through underwater plants, and put animals you find in a jar filled with pond water for study. Then return the animals to the water.

CHAPTER FIVE

ANIMAL DEFENSE MECHANISMS

Animals defend themselves in a variety of ways. Defense is crucial to ensure survival until as many young as possible have been produced.

Animals need to protect themselves from predators if they are to survive and breed. Some animals rely on speed to get away; others hide and blend into the background. Some have chemical defenses, while many animals that lack these chemicals pretend to have them. There are animals that protect themselves with physical defenses, such as horns and tusks. Some animals build protective structures, while others rely on behavioral adaptations to keep predators at bay.

Escape is often the best means of defense. A fleeing gazelle, for example, can run from all but the most agile predator. Many animals opt to escape into the air. Tiny animals called springtails launch themselves upward with a catapultlike appendage on their bodies. Most birds and insects can fly to safety, while flying lizards drop from the trees to glide from danger. Flying fish escape underwater predators by leaping above the

This Jackson's chameleon is a master of disguise. It can change the color of its skin to closely match its surroundings.

water and gliding, often for hundreds of feet.

CAMOUFLAGE

Other creatures prefer to hide from trouble. Their colors blend into the background, making them hard to see. This is called camouflage. Chameleons and cuttlefish can even change color to match their surroundings. Decorator crabs go one step further and actually become part of the scenery. They plant sea squirts and sea anemones on their shells to help them blend in.

Many birds also rely on camouflage. Bitterns live in reed beds. Their colors match the reeds closely. When the birds are startled, they stretch their necks upward to look even more like the plants that surround them.

A bittern stretches its neck to blend in with the reeds.

IMITATION

Some small animals hide by pretending to be objects. Many jumping spiders pretend to be bird droppings, jewel beetles look like drops of dew on a leaf, and leaf-hoppers look like thorns on a stem. Copying something else like this is called mimicry.

DISCOVERING MOTHS

In the day most moths hide away. Many hide on tree trunks and are camouflaged to blend in perfectly with the bark. The best way to see moths is to set up a light trap. Hang a white sheet in your backyard on a summer evening, and shine a flashlight on it from behind. As dusk falls, moths will land on the sheet. Take a look to see if you can spot any bark-hiding moths. After you have studied them, let the moths go in the same place that you caught them.

Warning coloration often includes bands of striking, contrasting colors. This is a blister beetle. Its colors warn predators that it contains corrosive chemicals that cause painful burns.

The champion mimics are stick and leaf insects. These animals are amazing mimics of leaves and other plant material. In addition to a leaf-shaped body some leaf insects have legs shaped like leaflets, and they sway their bodies just like a leaf in the breeze.

STINKY SKUNKS

Skunks are famous for the foul-smelling chemical spray they can produce when threatened. The skunk releases the chemicals, which can cause sickness and sting the eyes, from glands near its anus. The stinky spray can travel up to 9 feet (3m)!

DEFENSIVE CHEMICALS

Many small animals are protected by chemicals inside their bodies. They make the animal taste bad or make it poisonous. Some animals, such as stink bugs, are able to produce powerful smells.

Rather than hide away, chemically protected animals often advertise their bad taste with bright warning colors. Warning colors generally include yellows, reds, and black. Many animals, such as some poison arrow frogs, warn predators with bright blues and greens. A predator that eats a bad-tasting animal learns to avoid these warning colors in the future. Insects often get defensive chemicals from plants they eat when they are young. Monarch butterflies, for example, eat poisonous milkweed plants when they are caterpillars.

Some larger animals use defensive poisons too. When ribbed newts are threatened, they pierce their own skin with their poison-tipped ribs. The duck-billed platypus has small poison spurs on

When threatened, a ribbed newt can poke its sharp ribs through the row of tiny orange bumps running along its sides. The ribs are tipped with poison, making the animal an extremely unpleasant mouthful for any predator.

its hind legs. There is even a species of poisonous bird. The hooded pitohui from New Guinea has poison-coated feathers.

RESEMBLING POISONOUS ANIMALS

Some animals defend themselves by looking just like poisonous species. Biologists call this Batesian mimicry. Flatworms, sea slugs, and even fish mimic poisonous sea cucumbers, for example. Dangerous stinging animals, such as ants, wasps, and bees, also have many mimics. Harmless hover flies, for example, look just like wasps.

Sometimes, several different poisonous species share an almost identical coloration and pattern. This is called Müllerian mimicry. Many species of tropical butterflies are Müllerian mimics. If a predator takes a bite out of a poisonous butterfly, it will avoid all similar butterflies in the future. By sharing an easy-to-recognize coloration, all the Müllerian mimics profit from the protection gained by the predator's unpleasant experience.

GLUELIKE SECRETIONS

Some small animals use glues to stop attackers in their tracks. Threatened ladybugs squeeze blood from their leg joints. The sticky blood gums up enemies. Soldiers of one species of termite contain

DEVASTATING DISCHARGES

Bombardier beetles possess a powerful chemical defense. Rather than flying away from danger, these insects stand their ground. They aim their flexible anus at the enemy. Then, from a pair of glands inside, the beetles squirt a jet of boiling-hot corrosive chemicals. This lethal jet depends on an enzyme that is released with the chemicals by the beetle. Without the enzyme to drive the explosion the chemicals do not react.

MIMICRY

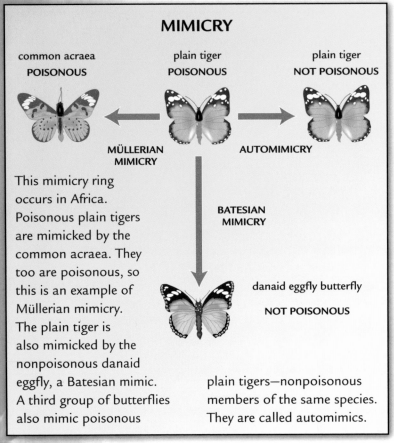

common acraea
POISONOUS

plain tiger
POISONOUS

plain tiger
NOT POISONOUS

**MÜLLERIAN
MIMICRY**

AUTOMIMICRY

**BATESIAN
MIMICRY**

danaid eggfly butterfly

NOT POISONOUS

This mimicry ring occurs in Africa. Poisonous plain tigers are mimicked by the common acraea. They too are poisonous, so this is an example of Müllerian mimicry. The plain tiger is also mimicked by the nonpoisonous danaid eggfly, a Batesian mimic. A third group of butterflies also mimic poisonous

plain tigers—nonpoisonous members of the same species. They are called automimics.

Velvet worms also use glue, but they spit it from their mouthparts.

DEFENSIVE SPITTING

Defensive spitting is not limited to glue. Some animals spit poisonous venom to ward off attackers. A spitting cobra rears up and drips venom from its fangs. It then breathes out hard to spray the venom at the enemy. Another spitter is the black fat-tailed scorpion. It squirts a jet of venom from the bulb at the tip of its long tail

Spiders, snakes, and other venomous animals do not generally use their venom to drive off attackers. Venom is used only as a last resort; a "dry" bite usually does the trick. However,

giant glue glands. During battle with an ant a soldier makes itself explode. Its violent death releases the glue, trapping the ant and allowing other termites to kill it.

WE'RE JAMMING

Bats find their way around by echolocating. They give out pulses of high-pitched sound and detect objects from the echoes. Bats prey heavily on moths, but some moths have tricks to avoid becoming a bat's dinner. A few species can confuse bats by emitting signals of their own. These sounds provide false echoes that jam the bats detection system. Other moths have scales on their wings that deflect the echolocation pulses. That allows the moths to escape detection in the same way that stealth aircraft avoid being found by enemy radar.

A SOUND DEFENSE

For some animals sound is just as important as color in defense. Madagascar hissing cockroaches squeeze out air to make a fierce hissing sound. One type of grasshopper, when grasped by a predator, lets out a powerful, high-pitched chirp. The sound shocks the predator into dropping the insect. Rattlesnakes (right) are venomous and do not wait to be attacked before sending out a warning sound. They shake horny scales on their tails to warn an enemy to keep well away.

some venomous animals are swift to give a deadly bite. Male Sydney funnel web spiders walk for miles through places full of predators in search of females to mate with. Male Sydney funnel web spiders have an extremely powerful venom at their disposal. They do not issue threats to enemies as many other spiders do; they simply kill anything that gets in their way.

BODY DEFENSES

Most animals defend themselves with physical defenses, including hairs, spines,

SHOCK TACTICS

Small birds are major predators of insects. Many moths, butterflies, leaf insects, and grasshoppers scare away these enemies with eye patches on their wings. When the insect unfolds its wings to reveal the eye patches, a small bird thinks it is facing a fearsome owl. The insect can fly away to safety in the confusion.

The moth's "eyes" mimic those of the owl. The moth's body may also mimic the owl's beak.

shells, and protective armor. When South American tarantulas are threatened, they shake their bodies quickly. That releases a cloud of fine hairs that irritate the nose and mouth of an attacker. Hairs have evolved into spines in many animals. Porcupines have an array of needle-sharp quills. Hedgehogs are also spiny. They have the added benefit of being able to roll themselves up into a ball.

Many animals with tough or spiky outer coverings roll up into a ball. That can present a wall of inpenetrable armor to a predator. Pill bugs roll up at the first sign of danger, as do armadillos. Tortoises draw their head and limbs into their tough shells.

STURDY SHELLS

Tortoise shells are based on modified rib bones. Many other animals have shells that are formed from chemicals drawn from water or food. Mussels and clams use powerful muscles to hold their shells closed tightly. Snails can draw their whole bodies into their shells, sealing the hole with a lid called an operculum. Nautilus shells are extra tough, both to deter predators and to withstand the enormous pressure in the ocean depths where they live.

A male Sydney funnel web spider raises itself ready to strike. The massive fangs can deliver enough venom to kill a small person.

Other animals have more active physical defenses. Deer and antelope have horns that can be used to deter predators. Horses and giraffes use their powerful hind legs to kick out, while hippos use their massive teeth to drive away other animals.

CONSTRUCTING OBSTACLES

Sometimes physical defenses are not enough, and animals put barriers in

LOSING LIMBS

Lizards such as skinks and geckoes have a remarkable defensive trick. When they are threatened, these lizards can make their tails drop off. The wriggling tail confuses the predator, allowing the lizard to get away. Losing body parts like this is called autotomy. Other animals can autotomize too; some salamanders, for example, can lose their toes.

UNBEATABLE DEFENSES

Sea cucumbers look like sausage-shaped blobs of jelly, but they have a series of incredible defenses. They can release stringy tubes that gum up an enemy, along with a cocktail of unpleasant chemicals. Sea cucumbers can transform their body from a solid into a more liquid state, then pour themselves into a tiny crack in the rocks to escape before toughening up again. And they can autotomize their entire gut to confuse a predator—and have the ability to quickly grow back these lost body parts. Sea cucumbers often advertise their amazing defenses with stunning colors and patterns.

place to keep predators at bay. Many insects form galls—bumps of plant tissue—under which they can drink plant sap in safety. Scale insects feed on the surface of plants, but coat themselves with a layer of tough wax. Spider mites spin silken webs to keep enemies out, while caddisfly larvae live inside protective cases they make from sand or gravel.

SMOKE SCREENS

When in danger, a squid releases an inky black liquid from a sac in its body. The liquid clouds the water, forming a smoke screen that allows the animal to escape. Squid ink is prized as a food coloring and flavoring in Mediterranean cooking.

Sea hares, a group of sea slugs, release a bright purple ink into the water when threatened. Their smoke screen is more of a warning, since sea hares are rich with poisons. Their ink warns enemies not to eat them.

This young lion is in danger of getting a muzzle full of sharp porcupine quills.

ANT BODYGUARDS

If your parents like gardening, they may know about tiny insects called aphids. These little bugs drink sap from plants, often in huge numbers. Take a closer look at some aphids on a plant. You may see some ants close by. They are not there to prey on the aphids but to protect them. Aphids secrete a liquid called honeydew that ants adore. In return for the honeydew ants protect the aphids against predators. Some even carry their aphids gently to safety at night or if enemies come near.

Confronted by a hungry predator, a pufferfish can quickly drink mouthfuls of water to expand its stomach and make itself look bigger and harder to swallow.

USING BEHAVIOR FOR PROTECTION

Other defensive strategies involve the ways animals behave. For many mimics it is not enough to just look like another animal; they must act like them as well. Drone flies mimic honeybees. The flies fly at the same speed as the bees and take off from flowers at exactly the same angle. Desert stink beetles stand on their heads and squirt foul-smelling liquid at enemies. Other desert beetles also stand on their heads to drive off predators, even though they do not have the liquid.

Size can also intimidate enemies. Cats arch their bodies and make their hair stand up when faced with a dog; toads and pufferfish can inflate their bodies, making them look bigger, fiercer, and more difficult to swallow.

A common behavioral defensive adaptation is herding. Herds often consist of several different species. On an east African savanna, for example, a

PLAYING POSSUM

Some animals fool attackers by pretending to be dead. When opossums are threatened, they lay limp and still with their mouths open. The defense works because many predators prefer to feast on freshly killed flesh. This behavior let to the phrase "playing possum." Hister beetles also play dead. They slide their antennae and legs into grooves that run along their bodies and wait for danger to pass.

PROTECTIVE PELLETS

Parasitic wasps are deadly enemies of burrowing spiders. They paralyze the spiders with their stingers, then lay an egg inside. When the egg hatches, the young wasp eats the still-living spider. Pellet spiders escape their wasp enemies with a neat defensive trick. A pellet spider makes a pear-shaped pellet of mud attached to a silk collar (right). When the spider is attacked, it pulls the collar so the pellet blocks the burrow, and the spider hides under it. The shape of the pellet stops the wasp from moving it; but when the danger has gone, the spider can roll it back again.

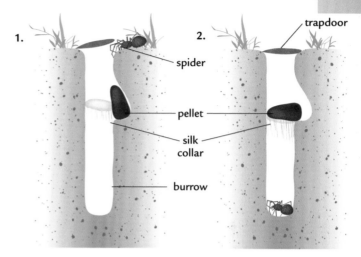

1. The silk collar is open, and the pellet is counterbalanced inside a pocket in the burrow wall.

2. The spider hides under the pellet which is pulled from its socket by tugging at the silk collar.

herd may contain wildebeest, gazelles, zebras, and ostriches. Animals form herds because many eyes are more likely to spot a predator than a solitary animal.

Herds are also better able to fight off attacks. Muskoxen form herds on the North American tundra. When attacked by a wolf pack, adult muskoxen form a circle around the young and drive off the wolves with their horns. Similarly, birds such as terns team up to drive away a crow or gull that comes too close to their nesting site. Owls, buzzards, and other birds of prey are often chased by groups of smaller birds, too—that is called mobbing.

HUMAN DEFENSES

Long ago in the past human ancestors were victims of predators just like any other animal. From tooth marks found on skulls scientists know that leopards preyed on our ancient ancestors, while the skeleton of a young 2-million-year-old Australopithecus is thought to be the remains of a large eagle's meal. Can you think of any defenses our ancestors might have had against such enemies?

CHAPTER SIX

MATING AND OFFSPRING

Animals exist to breed and produce young. They do so by attracting mates, driving off rivals, courting, and mating. Some animals look after their eggs and young too.

The most important part of any animal's life is reproduction. There are two ways to do this: asexual reproduction and sexual reproduction. Some animals that reproduce asexually, such as hydras, produce buds that grow from their bodies. The buds eventually break away to form a new animal.

These rose aphids were produced asexually.

ASEXUAL OR SEXUAL

Asexual reproduction allows populations to grow quickly. Also, an asexual reproducer passes 100 percent of her genes on, rather than half as in sexual reproduction. Yet the vast majority of animals reproduce sexually. Why is this?

The DNA (genetic code) of young produced sexually forms new combinations that differ from those of the parents. That leads to more genetic variety. This is important if a species has to evolve to cope with a new challenge, such as the appearance of a new parasite. Individuals that can survive the challenge produce young that can also survive. An asexual species might be wiped out before a response to the threat can evolve.

Some animals manage to get the best of both worlds. Aphids reproduce asexually in spring to increase numbers. Later generations in the fall reproduce sexually. They lay eggs that survive the winter before hatching in the spring.

Other animals, such as flatworms, can produce young by breaking off fragments. Each worm fragment grows into a complete new animal.

Other animals reproduce sexually. This involves male sex cells, or sperm, fertilizing (fusing with) female sex cells called eggs to produce young. Some animals, like slugs, contain both male and female sex organs and can reproduce with themselves. Animals like these are called hermaphrodites. Other animals, such as people, have separate sexes. Breeding is the process by which such animals find and mate with others, lay eggs or give birth, and sometimes care for their young.

FERTILIZATION

The eggs of many underwater animals are fertilized outside the body in the water. These creatures release sperm and eggs into the water, where they mix and fuse. The resulting young often drift for a time as plankton before settling on the sea bottom. The release of eggs and sperm is closely timed to minimize waste. The breeding cycles of many underwater worms, for example, are regulated by the phases of the moon. Other animals minimize waste further by fertilizing eggs inside the female's body. To do this, animals must attract a mate. Most animals then go through courtship. This allows the animals to indicate that each would make a good parent.

MATE COMPETITION

Animals attract distant mates by releasing chemicals into the air or by emitting

This giant clam is releasing its eggs into the water. This is called spawning. The eggs will fuse with sperm from other clams. The young will float among the plankton for a time before settling down on sand or coral rubble.

SWARMING LOVE BUGS

Small male midges get the most females, but things are different in love bugs. Female love bugs enter the swarms of males from the bottom. That allows the largest, heaviest male love bugs to grab the lion's share of mates. They are better able to drive off smaller males and occupy the lowest spots in the swarm, so they get the first chance to grab an approaching female.

loud sounds. Rivals can also be attracted by these signals. Males often gather to display to each other, with the victors getting the most mates. Many male insects form swarms, usually around a prominent object such as a tree stump or an overhanging branch. Females enter the swarm, pair up, and move away to mate. In midges smaller males usually win since they are agile and better able to grab the females.

Some male birds gather in similar groups at places called leks. Ruffs form leks on grasslands. During the breeding season the males grow spectacular collars of feathers. They use them to display to other males, along with aggressive dancing. Birds that lek often have vibrant colors. Cocks-of-the-rock are bright orange with large crests. Their leks take place on the rainforest floor.

DISPLAYS AND MATING

Most animals display to each other before mating takes place. These displays involve detailed movements as well as the release of chemicals. Some animals give their mates gifts. Some scorpion flies, for example, steal dead insects from spiderwebs and present them to females before mating. This is a risky business, and many males are caught by the spiders.

In fall and winter male ruffs are drab, but in spring they grow amazing feather collars used for display at leks.

PERILOUS MATING

Some female mantises eat their partners during mating (right). They eat the heads first, but the male is able to continue to mate. This may seem disastrous for the male, but his sacrifice is not in vain. His body provides a good food source for the female, allowing her to produce more eggs containing his genetic material. Such cannibalism usually occurs late in the season, when the males stand little chance of mating again. Earlier in the year they are more cautious.

Venomous animals such as spiders can have very complex displays. A male spider courts a female by plucking on her web. That lets her know that the male is a suitor and not an insect trapped on the sticky silk. Male scorpions grab the claws of the females and dance them back and forth.

Mating involves sperm moving from the male into the body of the female. This is done in a variety of ways. Male scorpions dance the female over a package of sperm laid on the ground, called a spermatophore, that enters her body along a duct. Spiders deposit sperm on a sheet of silk, then use a mouthpart to suck some up. This mouthpart is inserted into the female. Male bedbugs simply snip a hole into a female's body wall and dump a packet of sperm inside.

Birds and reptiles have a pair of organs called intromittent organs that guide the sperm into the female. Mammals have a similar organ called the penis. A male bee pops a mating structure called an endophallus out from his body. It enters the female through a duct in her body; once inside, sperm explodes out. Then the endophallus snaps away and blocks the duct. This stops other males from mating with the female later.

PRODUCING EGGS

Most animals lay eggs, with the young developing inside the eggs for a time before hatching. Many insects lay their eggs in a safe place close to a good food source before leaving them to survive alone. Mantis eggs develop inside a tough case called an ootheca, while lacewings lay their eggs at the end of long, flexible stalks to keep them away from foraging ants.

Some animals go to great lengths to care for their eggs and young. Earwigs dig small chambers in soil to lay their eggs in. They stay with the eggs, licking them to keep them free of fungi.

Many animals carry their eggs with them. Nursery-web spiders lay eggs in a tough case that they carry with their mouthparts. Male midwife toads wind strings of eggs between their feet, where they protect them and keep them moist. Some cichlid fish take their eggs, which are fertilized in

CHEATING COWBIRDS

Incubating eggs and raising young are hard work. Many birds, including honeyguides, cuckoos, and cowbirds, cheat by getting others to do the work for them. A cowbird sneaks into the nest of a small bird such as a finch or vireo. It lays a single egg before flying away. The hosts do not spot the intruding cowbird egg, despite the fact that it may look very different from those of the hosts. The cowbird chick is much bigger than its nestmates, and it hungrily gobbles down all the food that its foster parents can provide.

A yellow warbler struggles to feed a large cowbird chick as well as its own young.

the water, back into their bodies. They collect the eggs in their mouths, where they hatch and the young develop.

EGG INCUBATION

The eggs of many animals must be kept warm during development. Some, such as crocodiles, build a mound of decaying vegetation and lay their eggs inside. Rotting creates heat that keeps the eggs warm. Turtles bury eggs in warm sand, while the Maleo megapode bird lays eggs in holes in the soil. This bird relies on geothermal heat rising from deep underground. However, most birds incubate (keep warm) their eggs

PREGNANT MALES

Reproduction in sea horses is very unusual. After a lengthy courtship the female injects her eggs into a pouch in the male's body. There they are fertilized. The pouch wall grows around the eggs and acts like a placenta, nourishing the eggs. After a month of development the male gives birth to around 100 young. Unusually for fish, sea horses form pair bonds. Bonds are reinforced daily. The fish link tails, change color, and dance together.

Giant water bugs breed in an unusual way. A female attaches eggs to her mate's back with a waterproof glue. The male then provides all of the parental care for the eggs. This is extremely rare in the animal kingdom.

CROCODILE GENDER

Unlike people and most other animals, sex in crocodiles is not determined by genes inherited from parents. Instead, the temperature at which the eggs develop determines the sex of the young. Female Nile crocodiles incubate their eggs beneath mounds of rotting vegetation. If the average temperature during development is less than 89.1°F (31.7°C), the young become female. Between this and 94.1°F (34.5°C) the young become male, but above this temperature the young become female. Males occur over a range of only 5°F (2.8°C). As temperatures rise due to global warming, what do you think will happen to this species?

by sitting on them in a nest and warming them with their feathers. A female python incubates her eggs by coiling around them and vibrating her body. The heat generated by her muscles keeps the eggs warm.

BIRTH OF YOUNG

Many animals do not lay eggs at all. Instead, the eggs stay inside their bodies but hatch just before the young are born. However, the young get all the nourishment they need from food supplies inside the egg, not from the mother. Animals such as boas, manta rays, and pill bugs produce young in this way.

Most mammals also give birth to live young, although in this case there is no shelled egg from which they hatch. In marsupials such as koalas the young leave the

BROKEN WING TRICKERY

Birds go to great lengths to deter egg predators. Most build their nests high in trees. Ground-nesting birds are often camouflaged to blend in with their surroundings. Others use trickery. If a fox gets too close to a plover nest, the bird pretends to have a broken wing. Sensing an easy meal, the fox follows the plover. The bird leads the fox away from the nest. When it has covered a safe distance, the plover takes off and heads back to the nest.

body very early in their development. They climb into a pouch on the mother's body and attach to a teat to suckle milk.

In placental mammals, the group that includes humans, young leave the body at a much more advanced stage. Female placental mammals need to nourish their young inside their bodies. An organ, the placenta, grows to do so. Food and oxygen move through the placenta from the mother's blood, while waste products from the young go the other way. Some other animals, including velvet worms, sharks, and tsetse flies have an organ similar to a placenta for nourishing young.

HOW LONG INSIDE?

The time a young mammal spends developing inside its mother is called the gestation period. It is very short in marsupial mammals—around 30 days in kangaroos. At birth a baby kangaroo weighs around 0.04 oz. (1g). It climbs into a pouch on the mother's body and feeds on milk inside for another 235 days. Gestation period in placental mammals is related to size. Baby pygmy shrews are born after just 18 days of development. In African elephants the gestation period is around 23 months!

CARING FOR OFFSPRING

After giving birth, mammals feed their young with milk. Milk is produced by the mammary glands. It is full of nutrients that the young need to grow quickly. Milk varies in composition depending on the species. Seal milk, for

This baby sloth was nourished inside its mother via a placenta for six months before it was born. It will cling to its mother, feeding on milk, for a further four months. Then it will begin to eat leaves, and its mother will leave it to fend for itself in the canopy.

A seal produces milk rich in fats for her pup. This helps it lay down a layer of blubber that will keep it warm in cold polar waters.

animal food. Birds such as gulls carry food to their nests inside their crops. The birds regurgitate (vomit) food for the chicks to eat.

Incubating eggs and raising young usually requires two parents. One guards the nest; the other searches for food. Parent animals may reinforce their bond through displays. For example, while one albatross forages far and wide for food, the other stays at the nest to incubate.

When the parent birds swap roles, they perform incredible displays of honking, toe pointing, head shaking and bobbing, and bill clacking.

example, contains 60 percent fat. That helps the seal pup lay down a thick layer of blubber under its skin.

Mammals are the only animals that produce milk, although a few other animals feed their young with liquids from their bodies. Pigeons produce a nutritious liquid from their crops (part of the foregut). Flamingo chicks cannot filter food from water like the adults, and they too are fed a milky liquid from the parents' foregut.

Other animals that care for their young bring food to them from elsewhere. Carrion beetles protect their grubs until they molt. They feed them chewed up morsels of dead

IMPRINTING

For young animals the first few weeks of life are full of danger. It is vital for young to learn who their parents are. That helps young animals recognize who provides

MIGHTY MILK MAKERS

Although not as rich in fat as seal milk, whale milk is still highly nutritious. An adult female blue whale produces up to 50 gallons (200 liters) of milk daily to feed her calf. This vast quantity of milk enables phenomenal growth; a blue whale calf gains up to 97 lbs (44kg) in weight each day. After six months, when the calf moves on to solid food, the female blue whale may have lost more than 25 percent of her body weight.

PROBLEMS WITH IMPRINTING

Imprinting can cause problems, especially in captive-breeding programs to increase numbers of rare animals. Captive-bred California condors, for example, are fed by conservation workers wearing gloves shaped and colored just like an adult condor. Young condors are not exposed to humans at all. This keeps the rare youngsters from imprinting on people. Otherwise, the birds would not regard people as a threat after their release into the wild.

food and also helps the family group stay together later on. This important learning process is called imprinting.

Birds that leave the nest soon after hatching imprint on their mothers within a day or so of hatching. In animals that stay for a time in a nest or den, imprinting takes longer, around three weeks in wolf cubs, for example.

Adults learn to recognize the smell and sounds of their young too. That is important for animals such as penguins. Penguins must swim for many miles through open ocean to find food before returning to the rookery (breeding site). Rookeries are crowded, smelly, and noisy, yet a returning parent can still find its chick amid the chaos.

These ducklings will follow their mother everywhere. They imprinted on her at a very early age. This is important for ducks and other birds that leave the nest within just a few hours of hatching.

CHAPTER SEVEN

CLOSE ASSOCIATIONS AMONG ANIMALS

Animals constantly interact with other species. Many also live in groups with others of their own kind.

A bull moose wanders the North American forests alone. Occasionally he fights a rival male or mates with a female, but the rest of the time he keeps himself to himself. Moose are solitary (they live alone) and might not spend time with other moose, but they do carry around communities of fleas and lice. Any such relationship between species, such as the moose and its fleas, is called a symbiosis.

CLASSES OF SYMBIOSES

There are three types of symbioses. They are called mutualisms, commensalisms, and parasitisms. The relationship is called a mutualism if both species benefit. The Egyptian plover is a small bird that willingly hops inside the jaws of Nile crocodiles. The bird does not get eaten. That is because Egyptian plovers are crocodile dentists. They eat leeches and bits of meat that collect around the crocodile's teeth. The plover gets a meal, and the crocodile has its teeth cleaned.

Many animals share a close relationship with bacteria. During the day

An oxpecker picks fleas and ticks from a giraffe's hide. This is a mutualism—the giraffe benefits from the removal of pesky parasites, while the oxpeckers get an easy meal.

A TOUCHING STORY

Some shrimp share burrows in the sand with gobies (below). The shrimp do most of the work, building the burrow and keeping it clean and tidy. However, they are blind and depend on communication with the fish for survival. When outside the burrow, the shrimp keeps one of its antennae on the goby's tail. If danger approaches, the goby flicks its tail to warn its housemate. Fish and shrimp then dive for the safety of the burrow.

the bobtailed squid hides in sand on the seafloor. It comes out to feed at night. Swimming around on moonlit nights, it would cast a black silhouette against the sky, which a predator might spot. But the squid has a trick up its sleeve.

The squid has organs on its body that provide a home for bacteria. In return the bacteria produce light that shines downward from the squid. Without a silhouette the squid is cleverly camouflaged against the sky.

GETTING FRIENDS INSIDE

Many animals need tiny microorganisms in their guts to break down cellulose, a tough compound found in leaf material. Moving these tiny helpers into young, though, can be a problem. Koalas feed feces to their young to establish a bacteria colony inside. Termite nymphs (young) must feed on tiny drops of microorganism-rich liquid from the anus of an adult termite each time they molt. Molting removes the lining of the termite's gut, taking the essential microorganisms with it.

Birds such as egrets often follow elephants as they amble through grasslands. The birds feast on insects disturbed by the mammals' feet. The relationship between the birds and the elephants is a type of commensalism.

animal providing the taxi service is not harmed.

TROUBLESOME PARASITES

Some relationships see one animal suffering at the expense of another. They are called parasitisms. Virtually every animal species on earth suffers from parasites. Parasites live on the outer surface or inside the body of other organisms called hosts. Fleas, lice, ticks, tapeworms, flukes, and viruses are all types of parasites.

Most parasites get free food at the expense of their hosts. Fleas and ticks bite through the host's skin to suck blood. Aphids draw sap from the veins of plant leaves. Tapeworms live in the guts of

EXAMPLES OF COMMENSALISMS

Often one species benefits from an association, but the other is unaffected. This is called a commensalism. The remora fish has a very strong sucker, which it uses to attach itself to whales, sharks, and turtles. The remora gets a free ride and may feed on scraps of uneaten food, but the swimming

STRONG SUCKERS

Are you as strong as a remora fish? At the New York Aquariam scientists did an experiment to test the strength of a remora fish's sucker. They put a remora in a bucket of seawater, where it fastened itself to the side. They then lifted up the bucket of water by holding the remora's tail. One remora lifted 24 lbs (11kg)! Using a bucket of water and some bathroom scales, find out for yourself how much weight the remora fish was able to lift.

INVADING HOSTS BOTFLY-STYLE

Botfly larvae are parasites. Human botfly larvae, for example, develop inside hosts such as people. However, the adults are big, noisy insects that would quickly be spotted. How do these flies get their young to hosts without being caught in the act? Botflies are sneaky. They catch female mosquitoes in midair and attach their eggs to them before letting them go. When a mosquito lands on a person to feed, the eggs quickly hatch, and the young burrow into the skin.

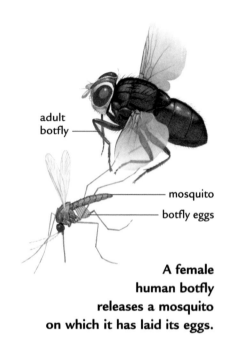

adult botfly

mosquito

botfly eggs

A female human botfly releases a mosquito on which it has laid its eggs.

their hosts and steal partly digested food, while tiny follicle mites sip oils that keep the host's skin supple.

This prairie dog is host for fleas. They may contain tiny creatures that cause a killer human disease called plague.

SPREADING TO HOSTS

One of the biggest problems parasites face is how to get from host to host. Tapeworm eggs need to be swallowed by a suitable host before they can develop in the host's gut. The chances of this happening for any one egg are very remote; tapeworms counter this by producing millions of eggs in their lifetimes.

Even an adult sheep botfly, which can easily get around by flying, has to deposit its young in a suitable spot. Female sheep botflies hover in front of a sheep's head.

WASPS OF DEATH

If you were a farmer, you wouldn't be too pleased to find bugs eating your crops. What would you do? One solution is to reduce pest numbers with killer parasites, called parasitoids. That is called biological control. Many parasitic wasps are parasitoids. These insects are good biological control agents since most target just one species of insect. The wasps lay eggs inside pests such as caterpillars and aphids. The eggs hatch, and the young wasps begin to munch their hosts' internal organs.

A parasitic wasp injected this tomato hornworm with eggs. When the eggs hatch into larvae, they will eat the hornworm.

When the host dies, the wasps become adult before emerging. Then they fly away to mate and find new hosts. The wasps help keep pest numbers under control.

They then shoot their bodies forward and squirt larvae (young) up the sheep's nose. The young live inside spaces in the sheep's head. After months of development the larvae drop back out through the nostrils to the soil. There they change into adults.

INJECTING HOSTS

Many parasites use carriers called vectors to get around. Mosquitoes are the vectors for parasites that cause the deadly disease malaria. When a mosquito drinks blood, some of the parasites move into the insect. There they develop for a time before moving to the mosquito's salivary glands. The parasites are injected into a new host when the mosquito bites another person.

ANIMALS AND GROUP LIVING

From shoals of silvery sardines to flocks of pink flamingos, many animals live with others of their species in groups. Like people, animals often live with relatives, while large groups may contain unrelated animals as well.

Group living can lead to competition for food and the spread of disease, but it does offer safety from predators. On African savannas herds of gazelle graze peacefully, but every few seconds a gazelle looks up and checks for signs of danger. With many pairs of eyes a large herd is more likely to spot stalking predators like lions or a cheetah. Other animals cooperate to rear young or hunt for food. Ostriches pool their chicks into one large group and work together to protect them. Pods of killer whales hunt porpoises in groups, and working as a team helps animals like lions, wolves, and African hunting dogs make their kills.

ANIMAL COLONIES

Some species have taken group living to the extreme. Animals such as corals, sponges, termites, and ants live in highly organized colonies where different individuals do different jobs. The Portuguese man-o'-war lives in the open ocean. It looks like a jellyfish and uses stinging tentacles to capture prey. But a Portuguese man o'-war is not one animal. It is a colony of hundreds of tiny individuals called polyps. The polyps come in different shapes and sizes depending on what function they carry out. A Portuguese man-o'-war colony has a polyp filled with gas to give buoyancy, polyps with stings that form tentacles, and others that digest food. A fourth type of polyp produces offspring.

This Portuguese man-o'-war is not one animal but a colony of separate polyps. Its tentacles contain powerful venoms that kill fish and other animal prey.

INSECT COLONIES

Social insects—termites, ants, and some bees and wasps—also live in closely related groups. They are among the most

FOR THE GOOD OF THE SPECIES

Biologists once thought that animals behaved for the good of the group or the species. In 1962 English zoologist Vero Wynne-Edwards (1906–1997) suggested that organisms controlled the rate at which they used up resources such as food, water, and space, and limited their birthrates to stop overpopulation. Later scientists realized that this idea is wrong. An animal that cheated by taking more than its fair share would be able to produce more offspring. The number of selfish animals would grow, until eventually every animal would be cheating the system. Behaving for the good of the species is not a stable strategy over long periods of time.

LOVE THY NEIGHBOR

Polyps in a Portuguese man-o'-war colony help each other survive because they are all sisters. Helping individuals that are not relatives is much rarer in the animal kingdom. But some animals do help others if they know the favor will be returned. Blood-drinking vampire bats live in dark caves with thousands of other bats. If vampire bats fail to find food, they quickly starve, so well-fed bats regurgitate blood for hungry neighbors (right). The well-fed bats do so because if they are ever hungry, the favor is repaid. Bats that cheat and do not give blood back when needed are ignored by the other bats and are more likely to die.

successful animals on Earth. There are more species of ants in one square mile of Brazilian rainforest than there are species of primates on the entire planet.

Generally, only one individual in a social insect nest produces young. She is the queen. Other members of the colony called workers forage for food, tend to the young, or defend the nest. Bee, ant, and wasp workers are always female. Males are produced only at the end of the season to fertilize the next generation of queens.

Groups of insects with particular jobs are known as castes, and

A dominant male gorilla (at right) is called a silverback. It fathers all of the young produced by the group.

THOUGHTS AND MINDS

People have what scientists call a "theory of mind." This means people can appreciate that others have their own minds, thoughts, feelings, and perspectives on events. People can know when someone else is hungry or in pain or understand a different point of view. It also enables some to lie and trick others into doing what they want. Scientists argue over whether the theory of mind applies to other animals. Chimpanzees, dogs, dolphins, and parrots (right) are very intelligent, but do they have thoughts and emotions like people do? What do you think?

they may have an appearance suited to their role. Some soldier ants have massive mouthparts for fighting. Others have plug-shaped heads used to block entrances to the nest. Termite soldiers have nozzle-shaped heads used for spraying defensive chemicals at their enemies.

PRIMATES

Most animals other than social insects reproduce independently and can survive without belonging to a group. But many still associate with their own kind. Primates, the closest relatives of people, live in a range of social groups. Marmosets are monogamous (one male mates with only one female). They live in small family units in which both sexes look after the young. Mountain gorillas live in harems. One enormous silverback male protects a group of females. The silverback mates with the females and fathers all the young.

Chimpanzees live in large troops of up to 80 individuals. Males and females may mate with several partners. Chimps from the same family tend to stick together within the group, but unrelated animals also form alliances. There are squabbles over food, mating, and grooming. Each animal has a social rank, which is crucial in deciding the outcome of disputes. Ancient human ancestors probably lived in societies similar to those of chimps. Later, they developed language to communicate complex information with other members of the group.

CHAPTER EIGHT

ANIMAL SYSTEMS OF COMMUNICATION

Communication is essential for fending off rivals, attracting a mate, warning others of danger, or showing them where to get food.

Animals are constantly communicating with each other. They have different reasons to communicate and different methods of communications too. Animals send out and receive signals using vision, touch, chemicals, and sound. Vision and touch are important at close quarters, while chemicals and sounds are more important over longer distances. Most animals use a combination of communication methods.

DEFENSE OF TERRITORIES

Many animals hold territories to ensure food supplies or to attract a mate. They mark their territories against rivals using signals. Birds, for example, defend their territories with song. Boundaries can also be marked out with chemicals. Tigers mark points on boundaries with chemical-laden urine. The message is reinforced by visual signals such as scratches on trees.

Visual signals are often used to drive off rivals. These

A Bengal tiger spray marks a tree. The tree forms part of the boundary of the tiger's territory. The urine that forms the spray contains chemicals that warn other tigers to keep away.

signals may take the form of displays. Honeypot ants, for example, scare away rival ants by walking stiffly on straight legs and making themselves look bigger.

BADGES AND DISPLAYS

Visual signals can also be animals' physical features, or badges. Badges include the antlers of deer, the feathers of a peacock's tail, and the red bellies of stickleback fish. These features are often a sign of dominance; dominant animals get more food and mates than other members of a group. Badges also indicate how good a mate an animal would be and help avoid fighting with other animals, which uses up energy and can sometimes lead to injury.

In Harris's sparrows, for example, dominance is related to the size of a black throat patch. Dominance can also depend on displays. A wolf holds its tail between its legs to indicate it is no threat to a dominant wolf with a higher-held tail. Dominance is important in social animals. Often only the dominant male and female will breed.

PHEROMONES AND THE USE OF SOUND

Visual communication is only useful at short range. To communicate over longer distances, many animals use chemicals

ELECTRIC CHATTER

Some animals are able to communicate in ways totally alien to people. Many fish, for example, can produce and detect electric fields. Electric eels use electric shocks to stun prey, but they also use their electric field to find their way around in dark river waters. Electric pulses are also used by these fish to communicate over short ranges with other electric eels.

The electric organs run along the body. They are composed of up to 200,000 electricity-producing disks. They can put out up to 500 volts—almost five times the voltage that comes from a wall socket.

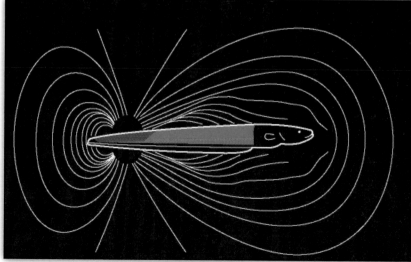

The white lines show the electric field that runs around an electric eel. The field is emitted from a region near the animal's tail. There are three electric organs. The main organ and Hunter's organ provide powerful bursts for defense and killing prey; Sach's organ releases a constant, low-intensity wave used for communication and navigation in murky waters.

■ Main organ

■ Hunter's organ

■ Sach's organ

called pheromones. Most male moths use their feathery antennae to detect pheromones released by the females. The chemicals invite the males to breed. A male sierra dome spider bundles a female's web into a ball as soon as he finds it. The web silk is rich with pheromones. By destroying the web, the male keeps other males from finding the female.

Sound is also important for long-distance contact. The calls of howler monkeys, for example, can be heard up to 3 miles (4.8km) away! Howler monkeys use these sounds to protect their feeding ranges from other monkey groups.

USING VIBRATIONS

Sounds, in the form of vibrations, can travel a long way through the ground

A DINNER INVITATION

Pheromones are not just used for mating but help many small animals form groups. Ticks feed on mammal blood. When a tick finds a good spot to feed, it releases a pheromone, and other ticks join it. The ticks release chemicals into the blood to keep it flowing and to stop it from clotting. More ticks mean more chemicals and less time spent feeding. This helps the ticks survive, since there is less chance of being discovered and removed by the host animal.

itself. In 2003 biologists found that elephants can tell if other elephants are in danger up to 10 miles (16km) away. They can detect tiny tremors in the ground caused by the movement of distant herds. The elephants receive the sounds through their feet. Whales are able to communicate with others over long distances by breaching; they jump out of the water and slam themselves down again.

ALARM SIGNALS

For animals that live in groups with close relatives it pays to warn them of danger. An aphid under attack from a ladybug will release alarm pheromones. They alert all the nearby aphids so they can escape. Sound is also used to alert others

One of the loudest sounds in the animal kingdom is produced by an adult howler monkey in full cry.

STOTTING TO SAFETY

Signaling to other species often depends on visual display. Fleeing gazelle often make very high bounds in the air. This is called stotting. Stotting indicates that the gazelle is fit, agile, and has already spotted the predator. A stalking cheetah is unlikely to waste time and energy chasing a stotting gazelle.

quickly. A rabbit thumps its foot on the ground to warn others before taking cover, while beavers slap their tails on the water's surface.

Warning communication is at its most sophisticated in primates. Vervet monkeys, for example, use different alarm calls depending on the nature of the threat. A loud cough warns of a leopard, two coughs indicate an eagle, while a chutter sound is given when a snake gets near.

COMMUNICATING WITH OTHERS

Animals regularly communicate with other species. Such communication usually acts as a warning to keep away, but sometimes communication helps both animals benefit. Honeyguides flash their white tail feathers at honey badgers to let them know they have found a beehive. The honey badger follows the bird to the hive. It breaks in with its strong claws to feast on the honey inside. The honeyguide eats the beeswax afterward. A relationship like this in which both partners benefit is called a mutualism.

INTRICATE COMMUNICATIONS

Some animals are able to communicate very complex information. Honeybees can tell their nest mates where nectar-rich

USING PHEROMONE TRAPS

Pheromones can sometimes be used to control pest animals. American freshwater crayfish were accidentally introduced to British waterways in the 1970s. American crayfish outcompeted the British crayfish for food and spread a disease that threatened to kill off their cousins. By setting up traps laced with the pheromones that American crayfish use to attract mates, scientists have been able to control the invaders.

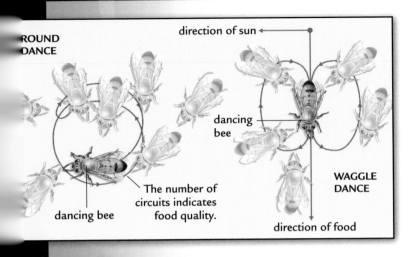

ROUND DANCE

direction of sun

dancing bee

WAGGLE DANCE

The number of circuits indicates food quality.

dancing bee

direction of food

Honeybees tell others where to find food by dancing. The other bees collect information by touching the dancer. The round dance lets the bees know about nearby food sources. The longer the dance, the richer the food source. To pass on information about food sources more than 165 feet (50 m) from the hive, bees move in a different way. That is called the waggle dance.

flowers are to be found (see above). Dolphins can also communicate complex information, using a range of squeaks, peeps, and whistles. Dolphins even have signature whistles. These distinctive sounds are used for identification, just like a person's name. Other dolphins learn them so the animals can address each other as they communicate.

The most complex of all communication systems is human language. Very little is understood of how or when language appeared, but our ancestors could talk by around 200,000 years ago. Speech required dramatic changes to the structure of the tongue and larynx and to the brain, but it opened up a world of possibilities to ancient peoples. They could coordinate hunts and send complex, abstract information between groups or through the generations.

CHUCKLING CANINES

Next time you play with your dog, listen closely to the sounds it makes. In 2003 biologists discovered that when dogs are playing, they laugh! The laughter sounds like panting to us, but it also contains low-frequency noises that people are unable to hear. These sounds communicate that the dogs are happy. Dog laughter is infectious too. Other dogs that hear it will try to join in the fun.

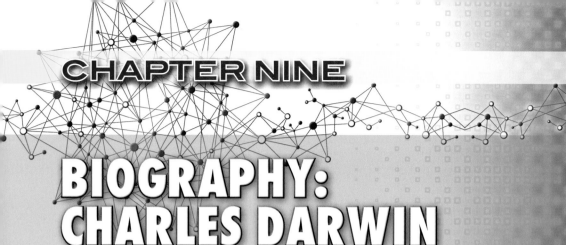

CHAPTER NINE

BIOGRAPHY: CHARLES DARWIN

Charles Darwin was born in Shrewsbury, England, on February 12, 1809. His father, Robert, was a respected physician. Charles's mother, Susannah, was the daughter of Josiah Wedgwood, the founder of the English porcelain industry.

In 1818, Charles started at Shrewsbury School, where his interest in science soon became evident. He went to study medicine at the University of Edinburgh in 1825, but he found he hated medicine. Darwin left Edinburgh in 1828 without taking a degree, and enrolled at Christ's College, Cambridge, to study theology. Once again, he found he was not greatly interested in the main subject of his studies but took the opportunity to develop his interest in scientific pursuits by joining a number of natural history societies. He got to know several eminent scientists at Cambridge, including John Henslow, professor of botany, and Adam Sedgwick, professor of geology. He was eager to learn from them and benefited greatly from their friendship. In the summer of 1831 Darwin accompanied Sedgwick on a three-week field excursion to Wales. The trip was the only time Darwin ever received formal scientific training.

George Richmond painted this portrait of Charles Darwin around 1840.

KEY DATES

1809	Born on February 12 in Shrewsbury, England
1825–28	Studies medicine at Edinburgh University
1828	Enters Christ's College, Cambridge, England, to study theology
1831	Appointed naturalist on HMS *Beagle*
1832–36	Travels in and around South America on *Beagle*
1839	Marries his cousin Emma Wedgwood in January; publishes *Journal of Researches into the Geology and Natural History of the Various Countries Visited by HMS Beagle...*
1842	Writes first, 35-page, draft of his evolutionary theory
1858	On June 18 receives an essay from naturalist Alfred Russel Wallace outlining Wallace's theory of natural selection; Darwin and Wallace present joint paper to the Linnean Society in London on July 1
1859	*On the Origin of Species by Means of Natural Selection* published on November 26
1871	Publication of *The Descent of Man, and Selection in Relation to Sex*
1882	Dies from heart attack on April 19; buried in Westminster Abbey

BRIGHT PROSPECTS

Darwin graduated in 1831 without plans to become a clergyman. In London, Robert Fitzroy, captain of HMS *Beagle*, was preparing an expedition to survey the coasts of South America for the Royal Navy. He asked the naval authorities to advertise for a naturalist to accompany him on the voyage.

Henslow advised Darwin to apply. On September 5, 1831, Darwin traveled to meet Fitzroy. They got on very well, and on December 27 the *Beagle* sailed from Portsmouth with Darwin on board.

GEOLOGY'S CHALLENGE TO BIBLICAL EVENTS

Until the 18th century, people believed that the Earth had been created literally as described in the Bible, that it was a few thousand rather than millions of years old, and that it had been shaped by events controlled by God. However, some scientists began to speculate that the Earth's history was much longer than had been supposed. In 1795 Scottish scientist James Hutton published his book *The Theory of the Earth*, in which he suggested that the Earth had changed very slowly over millions of years, and that it was still changing.

By the early 19th century Scottish geologist Charles Lyell had reached the same conclusion. Lyell and his supporters became known as the "uniformitarians," because of their theory that geological features changed uniformly.

0   600mi

Orinoco

VENEZUELA

British Guiana to Great Britain

Dutch Guiana to the Netherlands

French Guiana to France

COLOMBIA

Equator

ECUADOR

A N D E S

Galápagos Islands to Ecuador

BRAZIL

São Francisco

PERU

Callao

Bahia

Isla Pinta (Abingdon)

Isla Genovesa (Tower)

Isla Marchena (Bindloe)

Isla San Salvador (James)

Equator

Isla Fernandina (Narborough)

Isla Isabela (Albermarle)

Isla Santa Cruz (Indefatigable)

Isla San Cristóbal (Chatham)

Galápagos Islands

Isla Santa María (Charles)

Isla Española (Hood)

Lake Titicaca

BOLIVIA

Iquique

A N D E S

PARAGUAY

Paraná

Rio de Janeiro

Tropic of Capricorn

Copiapó

ARGENTINA

Pampas

Coquimbo

Santa Fe

URUGUAY

Mendoza

Mercedes

Valparaíso

Santiago

Buenos Aires

Montevideo

Concepción

Pampas

Valdivia

Bahia Blanca

Carmen de Patagones

Isla Grande de Chiloé

San Carlos

Patagonia

Puerto Deseado

Puerto Santa Cruz

Falkland Islands to Great Britain

Tierra del Fuego

In one of the most important scientific voyages ever made, from 1831 to 1836, HMS *Beagle* carried out an extensive survey of the South American coast (left) and also visited the Galápagos Islands (far left). The red line marks the ship's route.

This explained why rivers eroded valleys and the sea wore away cliffs. Hutton's and Lyell's theories met with strong resistance for many years; in fact, Darwin's friend Henslow suggested that Darwin read "but not believe" the recently published first volume of Lyell's book, *Principles of Geology* (1830).

CATALOGING THE GALÁPAGOS FINCHES

Ornithologist John Gould helped Darwin catalog his South American specimens. It was while Gould was preparing illustrations of the Galágapos finches that he is believed to have drawn Darwin's attention to the fact that they were not all variations of a single species, but belonged to distinct species. The main differences were in the shapes of their beaks.

To Darwin, it appeared that each of the islands had a distinctive group of species, and that these were related more closely to each other than they were to species on the mainland.

His explanation was that all the species were descended from a single, mainland species. Small land birds do not usually fly far, so their arrival from the mainland would have been a rare event, and there would have been no other finches or many other birds to compete with them on the islands. If there were no woodpeckers, a finch might develop the normal feeding habits of a wood-pecker, drilling out grubs in tree bark. Other finches might feed on seeds, nuts, or insects, without competing for these foodstuffs with other birds.

Over many generations, those birds with beaks most suitable for the particular food they ate survived and produced offspring, which inherited that type of beak. Gradually, a single original species evolved into several more. Although the finches provided strong confirmation of Darwin's theory of natural selection, he did not mention them in the first edition of the *Journal* or in *On the Origin of Species* (1859).

Geospiza strenua

This lithograph of John Gould's drawing depicts a pair of Galápagos finches. Darwin's studies of the Galápagos finches, now often called Darwin's finches, enabled him to formulate his theory of natural selection.

Darwin read the volume and was greatly impressed by it. What Darwin saw over the months and years of the *Beagle*'s trip soon persuaded him that Lyell's theories were correct.

LEMARCKISM

In the same way that Christians believed the biblical account of the age of the Earth, they also believed that God had created animals and plants, and that these remained exactly as God had created them.

French naturalist the Chevalier de Lamarck, in *Zoological Philosophy* (1809), proposed a way in which species might change; he developed the idea further in *Natural History of Invertebrate Animals*, published between 1815 and 1822. Lamarck suggested that, over many generations, species become increasingly well adapted to their environments; as that happens, they become slightly altered. He believed that the frequent use of an organ would gradually enlarge and strengthen it; lack of use would diminish and weaken it until it disappeared, and that these changes, through use or disuse, would be passed on to offspring. His theory is now called Lamarckism or "the inheritance of acquired characteristics." No instance of it has ever been found. Although Darwin's own theory was similar to Lamarck's, it contains some very significant differences and was developed from the actual observations Darwin made during his voyage on the *Beagle*.

THE GRAND VOYAGE OF DISCOVERY

In December 1831 the *Beagle* left port. When the *Beagle* made its first landfall in the Cape Verde Islands, off the coast of West Africa, Darwin was thrilled at his first sight of a volcanic island. The island's rock strata provided him with evidence to support the idea of slow change described in Lyell's book.

From here the *Beagle* crossed the Atlantic to Brazil, arriving in Bahía in February 1832. A tropical forest filled with orange, banana, and coconut trees surrounded the town. The boat sailed on down the Brazilian coast, landing at Rio de Janeiro on April 4, 1832.

Darwin spent far more time ashore than with the *Beagle* during the South American part of the trip. He was transfixed by everything he saw, from huge anthills to bright green parrots, from the smell of the cinnamon plants to the sound of howler monkeys. He collected hundreds of specimens, which he sent home to Henslow.

Next the *Beagle* set sail for Patagonia and Tierra del Fuego. At Punta Alta, Darwin found a cliff made up of shingle, gravel, and a layer of red clay. In this he discovered some enormous bones, which he realized must have belonged to creatures far bigger than any now in existence. He saw that they resembled similar modern, much smaller species, and wondered why the giant species had become extinct. He could think of no explanation that satisfied him, though.

TEMPESTUOUS DAYS

By early 1834 the *Beagle* was heading back to the Pacific through terrible storms. On July 22, 1834, they were relieved to reach Valparaíso, in Chile. Darwin set off to explore the Andes. When he found fossil seashells at 12,000 feet (3,658m), it confirmed the picture that had been forming in his mind: this part of South America must once have lain beneath the sea and later been pushed back up above sea level.

On February 20, 1835, a severe earthquake in Chile destroyed the city of Concepción. Darwin, who had been working at Valdivia, south of Concepción, noticed that the level of the land had risen after the earthquake and that a new island had emerged in the ocean close to the island group of Juan Fernández. To Darwin this was proof of his theory that land could rise up from the sea and eventually form mountain ranges.

In September 1835 the *Beagle* arrived in the Galápagos, a volcanic island group on the equator, nearly 500 miles (800km) from the coast of Ecuador. *Galápago* is the Spanish word for freshwater turtle, of which there were many on the islands. There were also several varieties of finches on the islands. Darwin collected as many specimens as he could and then thought no more about the finches until some time after he returned to London.

A HOMECOMING AND ACCLAIM

On October 2, 1836, a year after the *Beagle*'s visit to the Galápagos Islands, it arrived back in Portsmouth, southern England. Some of Darwin's geological reports had been published in journals while he was away, and he returned to England to find himself already recognized as a leading scientific figure.

On his return, Darwin went first to Cambridge, where he and Henslow began sorting the many specimens that Darwin had brought back. They also started to prepare Darwin's record of the voyage, which was published in 1839 as *Journal of Researches into the Geology and Natural History of the Various Countries Visited During the Voyage of* HMS *Beagle Round the World, under the Command of Capt. Fitzroy, R.N.*

Two giant tortoises stroll on Santa Cruz Island, in the Galápagos. When Darwin first encountered two Galápagos giant tortoises, he said one was eating a cactus, looked at him, and then strode away. The second hissed at him and then tucked its head into its giant shell.

DARWIN'S THEORY OF EVOLUTION

In 1837 Darwin moved to London. That year he also began work on the first of the many notebooks in which he gathered information about species.

In June 1842, Darwin wrote in pencil a first draft, 35 pages long, of what would become his theory of evolution by natural selection. Evolution is the gradual change in the characteristics of plants and animals over successive generations. Two years later Darwin wrote a second draft, this time in ink and 230 pages long. His attention then turned to revising the *Journal* for its second edition, and when that was done he wrote another book about his geological observations during the *Beagle*'s voyage. Darwin then spent several years studying barnacles. All the time, though, he continued to collect information about species. In 1857 he sent a draft of his written ideas to the American botanist Asa Gray. Darwin was not yet ready to publish this work, though.

JOINT CREDIT FOR A GRAND THEORY

He had written about half of the book by the middle of 1858, when on June 18 he received an essay written by the Welsh naturalist Alfred Russel Wallace. The two men had corresponded before, and Darwin realized that Wallace had reached exactly the same conclusion as he had about the way species evolve. Both men

had found that, within each species, some individuals have a characteristic (variation) that makes their survival more likely. They pass this feature on to their offspring, and gradually each generation that follows becomes more and more adapted to its particular environment. This was the theory of natural selection that Darwin worked out from his study of the Galápagos finches.

Although Darwin had formed his theory years earlier, his instinct was to let Wallace publish his findings first. Hutton and Lyell persuaded him to announce his theory at the same time, and eventually it was agreed that a "joint paper" would be presented to the Linnean Society in London on July 1, 1858.

Darwin's idea had been to publish his theory as a series of papers submitted to the society, but there proved to be too much material to make this practical. Instead, he prepared a popular, shortened account of his theory and published it in a book called *On the Origin of Species by Means of Natural Selection, or The Preservation of Favoured Races in the Struggle for Life*. The first edition, published on November 26, 1859, sold out on the first day.

DARWIN'S THEORY OF EVOLUTION BY NATURAL SELECTION

When scientists speak of "the theory of evolution," the theory they have in mind is that put forward by Darwin and

In 1859, Darwin wrote this draft title page of "An Abstract of an Essay on the Origin of Species and Varieties through Natural Selection."

Wallace, in which natural selection is the mechanism that drives forward the evolution of species. Evolution itself is not a theory, it is a fact, and one that has been observed happening many times. It is the descent of organisms from generation to generation with slight modification until they are so different from their ancestors that they make up a new species.

WITHSTANDING THE PUBLIC BACKLASH

Although Darwin had deliberately avoided the question of human evolution in *On the Origin of Species*, his theory of natural selection was disturbing to many. Religious opponents criticized it for implying that the higher powers of humans have developed naturally from characteristics already present in animals, thereby denying the belief that God has placed humans above the animals. Darwin continued to develop his theory, discussing human origins in *The Descent of Man, and Selection in Relation to Sex* (1871). He also wrote several other books on natural history.

Charles Darwin was a gentle, modest man, who held liberal views on social matters. He married his first cousin Emma Wedgwood in 1839 and the couple had 10 children. For most of his life, he suffered from intermittent symptoms of sickness that made him a semi-invalid; no one is quite sure of the cause. Darwin died on April 19, 1882, and was buried in Westminster Abbey, London.

SCIENTIFIC BACKGROUND

Before 1820

Scottish scientist James Hutton (1725–1797) argues that the Earth is millions of years old

Darwin's grandfather, Erasmus Darwin (1731–1802), suggests that species might be transformable

French naturalist the Chevalier de Lamarck (1744–1829) proposes that species can inherit characteristics acquired by the previous generation

English clergyman Thomas Malthus (1766–1834) writes an *Essay on Population* in which he maintains that a struggle for survival in populations is inevitable

1820

1820–40 English geologists William Buckland (1784–1836) and Adam Sedgwick (1785–1873) develop their "catastrophist" view of geological history

1827 French mathematician Jean Baptiste Fourier (1768–1830) suggests that human activities have an effect on the Earth's climate

1830

1831 Darwin sets sail with Captain Robert Fitzroy on HMS *Beagle* as the expedition's unpaid naturalist

1835 Darwin makes important discoveries about the evolution of species on the Galápagos Islands

1839 Darwin publishes his *Journal of Researches into the Geology and Natural History of the Various Countries Visited by HMS* Beagle

1837 Darwin reads Thomas Malthus's *Essay on Population*

1840

1842 Darwin writes the first draft of his theory of evolution

1844 Robert Chambers (1802–1871) publishes anonymously his theory of the development of species in *Vestiges of Creation*

1848–52 Welsh botanist Alfred Russel Wallace (1823–1913) collects specimens in South America

1850

1854–62 Wallace travels to the Malay archipelago and the East Indies (now Indonesia), and collects more than 125,000 specimens

1858 Darwin and Wallace present a joint paper on their theory of natural selection to the Linnean Society in London; in 1859 Darwin publishes *On the Origin of Species by Natural Selection*

1858 Wallace reads Malthus's *Essay on Population* and forms theory of "survival of the fittest," which he sends to Darwin

1860

1863 British geologist Charles Lyell (1797–1875) and British zoologist Thomas Huxley (1825–1895) publish *Antiquity of Man* and *Man's Place in Nature*

1865 Austrian botanist Gregor Mendel (1822–1884) publishes his theory of a law of inheritance, but it does not gain much attention until 1900

1869–1910 Darwin's cousin Francis Galton (1822–1911) develops eugenics, the breeding of human beings for evolutionary improvement

1870

1871 Darwin's work *The Descent of Man* concludes that man evolved from apelike ancestors in Africa

1871 A prehistoric pterodactyl skeleton is identified by the first American paleontologist, Othniel Charles Marsh (1831–1899)

1880 French chemist Louis Pasteur (1822–1895) develops the germ theory of disease

1880

1887 Belgian cytologist Eduard van Beneden (1817–1910) discovers that each species has a fixed number of chromosomes

1889 Wallace publishes *Darwinism* and receives the first Darwin Medal

1890

After 1890

1890–96 "Lamarckism" rejected by German biologist August Weismann (1834–1919)

1902 American geneticist Walter Stanborough Sutton (1877–1916) states that chromosomes are paired and may be the carriers of heredity

1900 Mendel's theory of inheritance is revived

POLITICAL AND CULTURAL BACKGROUND

1815 After his defeat at the Battle of Waterloo, French emperor Napoleon Bonaparte (1769–1821) throws himself on the mercy of the British but is banished to the island of Saint Helena in the south Atlantic Ocean

1824 German composer Ludwig van Beethoven (1770–1827) completes his *Mass in D Major*

1826 American novelist James Fenimore Cooper (1789–1851) publishes *The Last of the Mohicans,* one of a series of novels by Cooper that take pioneer and American Indian life as their subject

1827 *An American Dictionary of the English Language* is published after 28 years of work by American lexicographer Noah Webster (1758–1843)

1837 American inventor Samuel Finley Breese Morse (1791–1872) patents his version of the telegraph, a machine that sends letters in code

1837 In Britain, Queen Victoria (1819–1901) comes to the throne. She will rule for the rest of the 19th century, and until her death in 1901

1844 American inventor Charles Goodyear (1800–60) treats rubber with sulfur under heat and pressure to make it more elastic and strong; the process, known as "vulcanizing," allows the development of the rubber tires for which he becomes famous

1846 Famine sweeps Ireland as the potato crop fails

1850 German chemist and physicist Robert Wilhelm Bunsen (1811–1899) invents the Bunsen burner

1850 Bavarian-American entrepreneur Levi Strauss (1829–1902) introduces "bibless overalls," the forerunner of denim jeans, for miners in California

1859 American landscape painter Frederick E. Church (1826–1900) completes *Heart of the Andes*

1867 German social, political, and economic theorist Karl Marx (1818–1883) publishes *Das Kapital*, in which he develops the theory of the evolution of society

1865 The American Civil War ends, President Lincoln is assassinated, and a 12-year "Era of Reconstruction" begins in the South

1870 The Vatican Council votes that the pope is infallible when defining doctrines of faith or morals

1877 The disputed 1876 election for the U.S. presidency is resolved when an electoral committee declares in favor of the Republican Rutherford B. Hayes (1822–1893)

1884 American writer Mark Twain (1835–1910) publishes *The Adventures of Huckleberry Finn*. The author takes his pen-name from the phrase used by men testing depths in shallow rivers: "mark twain" means that the mark shows the river is two fathoms deep

1886 In the United States, Coca-Cola goes on sale for the first time. Made by an Atlanta chemist, its ingredients include South American coca and African kola nuts

1893 A four-year economic depression begins in the United States. On June 27 the Wall Street stock market collapses as share prices plummet

airfoil A surface that creates a force (lift) that allows animals to glide or fly.

antenna One of a pair of sensitive feelers on the heads of insects and many other invertebrates.

asexual reproduction Production of young without the need for mating or the fusion of sex cells.

automimic Animal that mimics another member of its own species.

autotomy The loss of a limb or tail to fool a predator.

Batesian mimic Nonpoisonous animal that looks like a different, poisonous species.

biological control The use of parasitoids and predators to control pests.

blubber Layer of fat deposits just beneath the skin of animals like whales, seals, and penguins.

breaching When a whale leaps from the water and smashes its body down again to communicate with sound over long distances.

camouflage A pattern of coloration that allows an animal to blend in with its surroundings.

carnivore Animal that catches other animals for food.

cellulose Chemical that forms tough molecules in the walls of plant cells.

colonial animal Animal formed by a number of separate individuals.

commensalism Relationship between organisms in which one benefits and the other (the host) is unaffected.

compound eye Insect eye composed of many individual lenses.

courtship Display between a male and a female prior to mating.

deoxyribonucleic acid (DNA) Molecule that contains the genetic code for all cellular (nonvirus) organisms.

detritivore Animal that feeds on dead animal or plant material.

drag Force that opposes the movement of an object through water or air.

echolocation Use of sound to detect objects in the dark by animals like bats, dolphins, and some seals and shrews.

enzyme Protein that speeds up chemical reactions in organisms.

estivation To spend periods of dry weather in inactive state.

exoskeleton Tough outer skin of animals such as insects.

fertilization The fusion of a sperm with an egg.

filter feeder Animal that sieves fine particles from water for food.

gait The way an animal moves.

gene Section of DNA that codes for the structure of a protein.

gestation period The time an animal spends developing inside its mother.

habitat The type of place in which an organism lives.

herbivore Animal that feeds on plants.

hermaphrodite Animal with both male and female sexual organs.

hibernation To spend the winter in an inactive or dormant state.

honeydew Sugary fluid released by aphids.

host Organism attacked by a parasite or unaffected in a commensalism.

hydrostatic skeleton A fluid-filled structure used as a brace for muscles in
many invertebrates.

imprinting Attachment of young birds
and mammals to their mother after
birth.

incubation Keeping young birds warm
on the nest.

invertebrate Animal that does not have
a backbone.

larva The young of certain types of
insects.

lek Place where males of certain species
compete for mates.

lift Upward force produced by airflow
over a wing.

migration Long-distance journey by animals such as birds to warmer places
during winter weather.

mimicry Imitation of an object or
another animal.

mobbing When small birds team up to
drive away predators or egg thieves.

molt The shedding of an animal's outer
skin; creatures like insects and spiders must molt to grow.

mucus Sticky fluid.

Müllerian mimic Poisonous animal that
mimics (looks like) a poisonous
member of a different species.

mutualism A relationship to the mutual
benefit of two or more species.

nectar Sweet liquid used by plants to
tempt pollinating animals.

neurotoxin Chemical in some venoms
that blocks a victim's nervous
system.

nocturnal Active at night

omnivore Animal that eats both plant
and animal matter.

ootheca Egg-case of insects such as
mantises.

parasitism Relationship in which one
organism benefits at the expense of
another.

parasitoid A parasite that eventually
kills its host.

pheromone Chemical released by an animal to attract, warn, or ward off
others of the same species.

placenta Organ that develops during
pregnancy and supplies the growing
young with food and oxygen, and
takes away waste.

plankton Tiny animals, often the young
of larger creatures, that float in the
surface waters of the ocean.

polyp Individual member of a colonial
animal, such as coral or a
siphonophore.

predator Animal that catches other animals for food.

prey Animal caught and eaten by
another animal.

resilin Chemical with elastic properties
that occurs in the skins of insects.

rookery Breeding ground of penguins
and other birds.

sessile Animal that does not move during its adult life.

sexual reproduction Production of
young through the fusion of sex
cells, often after mating between a
male and a female.

spermatophore A package that contains
sperm.

stotting When antelope jump high to display to a predator.

surface tension Property of water that gives it a thin, elastic "skin."

symbiosis A relationship between different organisms.

tracheal system An insect's breathing system.

vectors An animal that carries a parasite between hosts.

venom A poison delivered by a predatory animal to immobilize prey.

vertebrate Animal that has a backbone.

vortex A swirl of air that rolls from the wings of a flying or gliding animal.

Beaty Biodiversity Museum
2212 Main Mall
Vancouver, BC V6T 1Z4
Canada
(604) 827-4955
Web site: http://beatymuseum.ubc.ca
This museum is dedicated to natural history collections and provides exhibits of such treasures as a blue whale skeleton, fish, insects, mammals, birds, reptiles, amphibians, and plants from Canada and worldwide.

Canadian Museum of Nature
P.O. Box 3443, Station D
Ottawa, ON K1P 6P4
Canada
(613) 566-4700
Web site: http://nature.ca
The Canadian Museum of Nature has more than ten million specimens from Earth's history. Its collections include botany, vertebrates, invertebrates, and earth sciences.

Cincinnati Zoo & Botanical Garden
3400 Vine Street
Cincinnati, OH 45220
(513) 281-4700
(800) 94-HIPPO (944-4776)
Web site: http://cincinnatizoo.org
This zoo was designated as a National Historic Landmark in 1987. It is acclaimed for its dedication to conservation, education, and preservation of wild animals and wild spaces.

Down House
Home of Charles Darwin
Luxted Road
Downe, Kent BR6 7JT
England
0 1689 859119
Web site: http://www.english-heritage. org.uk/daysout/properties/ home-of-charles-dawin-down-house
Down House was the home of Charles Darwin and is one of the key visitor attractions near London. There are twilight tours of the property and lecture series on Darwin, his family, studies, and collections.

Essig Museum of Entomology
1101 Valley Life Sciences Building, #4780
University of California, Berkeley
Berkeley, CA 94720
(510) 643-0804
Web site: http://essig.berkeley.edu
This museum has an acclaimed terrestrial arthropod collection, particularly in the insect fauna of California. It is open to the public only on Cal Day and on Darwin Day (on Darwin's birthday).

The Field Museum
1400 South Lake Shore Drive
Chicago, IL 60605-2496
(312) 922-9410
Web site: http://fieldmuseum.org
The Field Museum educates the public about the diversity and relationships in nature and among cultures. Its encyclopedic collections contain

biological and geological specimens in the areas of anthropology, botany, geology, paleontology, and zoology.

National Museum of Natural History
Smithsonian Institution
P.O. Box 37012
Washington, DC 20013-7012
(202) 633-1000
Web site: http://www.mnh.si.edu
This museum's collections examine ancient life forms, rare gemstones, and more than 126 million natural science specimens and cultural artifacts. Its science departments include anthropology, botany, entomology, invertebrate zoology, mineral sciences, paleobiology, and vertebrate zoology.

Natural Science Center of Greensboro
4301 Lawndale Drive
Greensboro, NC 27455
(336) 288-3769
Web site: http://www.natsci.org
This center offers the public a hands-on learning experience about the natural world. It provides exhibits, galleries, a herpetarium, an aquatics lab, a reptile lab, a robotics lab, a mineral lab, an insect lab, and a zoo.

Wildlife Conservation Society
2300 Southern Boulevard
Bronx, NY 10460
(718) 220-5100
Web site: http://www.wcs.org

This society saves wildlife and natural places worldwide. It manages the largest system of urban wildlife parks, including the Bronx Zoo, New York Aquarium, Central Park Zoo, Prospect Park Zoo, and Queens Zoo.

WEB SITES

Due to the changing nature of Internet links, Rosen Publishing has developed an online list of Web sites related to the subject of this book. This site is updated regularly. Please use this link to access the list:

http://www.rosenlinks.com/CORE/Anima

Allaby, Michael. *Animals: From Mythology to Zoology* (Discovering the Earth). New York, NY: Facts On File, 2010.

American Museum of Natural History. *Animal Life: Secrets of the Animal World Revealed*. New York, NY: DK Publishing, 2011.

Burnie, David. *Animal: The Definitive Guide to the World's Wildlife*. New York, NY: DK Publishing, 2005.

Casper, Animals: *Creatures That Roam the Planet* (Natural Resources). New York, NY: Chelsea House Publishers, 2007.

Darwin, Charles. *The Variation of Animals and Plants Under Domestication*. Vols. 1 and 2. Nabu Press, 2010.

Dunn, Jon L., and Jonathan Alderfer. *National Geographic Field Guide to the Birds of North America*. 5th ed. Washington, DC: National Geographic, 2006.

Gibson, J. Phil, and Terri R. Gibson. *Natural Selection* (Science Foundations). New York, NY: Chelsea House Publishers, 2009.

Haskell, David George. *The Forest Unseen: A Year's Watch in Nature*. New York, NY: Viking Penguin, 2012.

Heiligman, Deborah. *Charles and Emma: The Darwins' Leap of Faith*. New York, NY: Henry Holt, 2009.

Hollar, Sherman, ed. *A Closer Look at the Animal Kingdom* (Introduction to Biology). New York, NY: Rosen Publishing, 2012.

King, David C. *Charles Darwin* (DK Biography). New York, NY: DK Publishing, 2006.

Krull, Kathleen. *Charles Darwin* (Giants of Science). New York, NY: Viking, 2010.

Leone, Bruno. *Origin: The Story of Charles Darwin* (Profiles in Science). Greensboro, NC: Morgan Reynolds Publishing, 2009.

Meyer, Carolyn. *The True Adventures of Charley Darwin*. Boston, MA, and New York, NY: Harcourt, 2009.

O'Shea, Mark. *Reptiles and Amphibians* (DK Handbooks). New York, NY: 2010.

Panno, Joseph. *Animal Cloning: The Science of Nuclear Transfer* (New Biology). Rev. ed. New York, NY: Facts On File, 2010.

Siwanowicz, Igor. *Animals Up Close*. New York, NY: DK Publishing, 2009.

Spicer, John I. *Biodiversity* (World Issues Today). New York, NY: Rosen Publishing, 2009.

PHOTO CREDITS